pictorial guide to
perennials

by
M. Jane Coleman Helmer, Ph.D.
Karla S. Decker Hodge, B.S.

Third Edition 2001
Second Printing July 2001

ISBN 0-89484-037-1

Merchants Publishing Company
20 Mills Street, Kalamazoo, Michigan 49001

Printed in United States of America

contents

LISTS: PERENNIALS FOR SPECIAL SITUATIONS AND USES

acknowledgments

The authors wish to thank the following companies and individuals for their kind cooperation in providing information, encouragement, and advice throughout the preparation of this book:

    Personnel at The Bailey Hortorium, Cornell University, Ithaca, NY: Consultants
    Mary Walters, Walters Gardens, Inc., Zeeland, Michigan: Consultant
    Ben J. Behrman, Merchants Publishing Company: Art Direction

Photographs are from Merchants' comprehensive library of horticultural subjects and from the following sources: Argo Studios, Bluestone Perennials, Dean Clark, Dan Flotterud, Peter Lindtner, Muriel Orans, Ben Pirrone, Dale VanEck, Walters Gardens, Inc., Westland Photography and Photostudio Visions B.V.

introduction

Perennials are among the most useful plants for the home landscape. They are colorful and diverse, and can be used as more or less permanent features. While trees and shrubs — woody perennials — provide the outline and backdrop of the landscape, non-woody perennials provide more detail, interest, and seasonal accents.

These plants, which are often called herbaceous or hardy perennials, come up year after year. Their life spans vary from just a few seasons to a decade or longer. Notable for their durability are Chinese peonies *(Paeonia lactiflora)*, a clump of which may flourish for 30 years. Among the short-lived perennials are delphinium hybrids, which are spectacular for several seasons but which eventually lose vigor and need to be replaced. The beauty of their blooms and the plants' screening qualities make delphiniums well worth replacing every few years.

Many perennials described in this book are truly herbaceous, dying to the ground and growing fresh tops each spring from roots and stems that overwinter in the soil. Both Chinese peonies and delphiniums, as well as the majority of garden daisies (species of *Anthemis, Aster, Chrysanthemum, Coreopsis, Doronicum, Erigeron, Gaillardia, Heliopsis, Rudbeckia)* are examples of perennial herbs whose tops die completely in most zones.

Other perennials, such as moss phlox *(Phlox subulata)* and periwinkle *(Vinca),* have woody stems that often survive winter freezes and from which fresh growth appears in spring. Still others, including coral bells *(Heuchera)* and heartleaf bergenia *(Bergenia cordifolia),* display their attractive foliage throughout the winter months. In southern zones, herbaceous perennials such as columbine *(Aquilegia)* retain their foliage through most or all of the winter.

Diverse colors, styles

Probably no other group of plants is represented by the extensive range of height, spread, and flower and foliage forms that can be found among perennials. Some grow to a stately 8 feet (2.4 meters) or more, while others creep over the ground, growing just 3-4 inches (8-10 centimeters) high. The clumps may spread, mound, or sprawl, or they may remain relatively narrow and concise year after year. Between these extremes is a myriad of varying shapes and sizes.

Flowers are produced in almost all colors of the rainbow, with a variety of forms and shapes. Some grow as tall spikes; others are in daisy form. Star, bell, globe, tube, powderpuff, spider, and variations of these bloom shapes create interest in the garden from early spring until frost.

Foliage styles range from the simple grasslike leaves of garden pinks *(Dianthus)* to the more complex, lobed,

and deeply cut leaves of Shasta daisy *(Leucanthemum* X*superbum)*. Nearly every shade of green is represented, sometimes with variegations that stripe, edge, or mottle the leaves with gold or ivory for a two-tone effect. Such foliage gives plants ornamental value before and after flowering, and a number of perennials are grown purely for their foliage quality.

Cultural needs vary

Today's perennials have their origins in nearly all parts of the world. The different soils and climates in which they can be grown are as varied as their origins. Although some are relatively specific as to their need for, say, well-drained soil or winter temperature tolerance, many perennials are very adaptable and will grow in a broad range of conditions. These and other details are in the plant descriptions on pages 25-166.

Perennials for all gardens

Perennials need relatively little maintenance. While annuals must be planted afresh each year, many perennials come up year after year with minimal or no added work. A single clump of speedwell *(Veronica)*, planted as an accent, will flourish for years, undemanding, persistent, and reliable. Low maintenance groundcovers, such as bishop's-weed *(Aegopodium)* and lamb's ears *(Stachys)*, are especially good in a natural landscape planting; they maintain their vigor without being so invasive that they dominate and crowd out other plants. In more formal perennial plantings, maintenance requirements become greater: plants may need support or trimming, vigorous roots should be divided periodically, and tender favorites like dahlias must be lifted and stored each winter.

Perennials as accents

Accent plantings are needed in every landscape that would otherwise be lacking in any significant features. The range of color, size, and style means there is usually at least one perennial for every situation — whether it be a balcony container or the focus of massed plantings, the end of a vegetable garden that's seen from the living room, or the rough stony ground at one corner of the property.

Accent perennials are frequently used in combination plantings: a tall shrubby perennial with some other landscape feature such as a fence, or in a planting containing a small tree, shrub and/or conifer. Adam's needle *(Yucca filamentosa)* and black-eyed Susan *(Rudbeckia)* are examples; these perennials also stand out well as solitary accents. Baby's breath *(Gypsophila)*, with its cloud-like show of blossoms, makes a welcome contrast to conifers. And in areas where it's winter hardy, a clump of pampas grass *(Cortaderia selloana)* makes a stately specimen planting.

Rudbeckia fulgida

garden fragrance

Foliage as well as flowers can provide fragrance. Perennials with aromatic foliage are indicated (F) in the following list.

Adenophora Ladybells
Anthemis Golden Marguerite (F)
Arabis Rock Cress
Artemisia Wormwood (F)
Buddleia Butterfly Bush
Calamintha Calamint (F)
Centranthus Valerian
Chamaemelum nobile
   Roman Chamomile
Chrysanthemum (F)
Cimicifuga Bugbane
Clematis recta Ground Clematis
Clematis terniflora
   Sweet Autumn Clematis
Convallaria majalis
   Lily-of-the-valley
Crambe Colewort, Sea Kale

Dennstaedtia punctiloba
   Hay-scented Fern (F)
Dianthus
   Pink, Carnation, Sweet William
Dictamnus albus Gas Plant
Erysimum cheiri English Wallflower
Filipendula Meadowsweet
Galium odoratum
   Sweet Woodruff (F)
Hemerocallis (some) Daylily
Hesperis matronalis Dame's-rocket
Hosta (some) Plantain Lily
Iris (some) Bearded Iris
Lavandula angustifolia
   English Lavender (F)
Lilium Lily
Lysimachia nummularia
   Creeping Jenny
Lunaria annua Honesty
Melissa officinalis Lemon Balm (F)
Mentha Mint (F)
Monarda Wild Bergamot (F)
Nepeta Catmint (F)

Oenothera
   Evening Primrose, Sundrops
Origanum vulgare Marjoram (F)
Pachysandra terminalis
   Japanese Spurge
Paeonia Peony
Papaver (some) Poppy
Perovskia atriplicifolia
   Azure Sage (F)
Phlox (some)
Polygonum aubertii
   Silver Fleece Vine
Primula Primrose
Rosmarinus officinalis Rosemary (F)
Ruta graveolens Rue (F)
Salvia Sage (F)
Santolina chamaecyparissus
   Lavender Cotton (F)
Satureja montana Winter Savory (F)
Teucrium chamaedrys
   Wall Germander (F)
Thymus Thyme (F)
Viola odorata Sweet Violet

Sedum 'Matrona'

perennials for containers

Achillea, shorter selections Yarrow
Aconitum Monkshood
Ajania pacifica
    Silver-and-Gold Chrysanthemum
Anemone Xhybrida Windflower
Anthemis Golden Marguerite
Aquilegia Columbine
Artemisia Dusty Miller
Aster spp Aster
Campanula poscharskyana
    Serbian Bellflower
Canna hybrids Dwarf Canna Lily
Carex
    Silver Variegated Japanese Sedge
Centaurea montana Mountain Bluet
Cheiranthus cheiri
    English Wallflower
Chrysanthemum (shorter varieties)
Dahlia (smaller varieties)
Dianthus
    Pink, Carnation, Sweet William
Dicentra Bleeding-heart
Doronicum Leopard's-bane
Erysimum cheiri English Wallflower
Festuca glauca cvs Blue Fescue
Fragaria
    Strawberry, ornamental & fruiting
Gaillardia Xgrandiflora
    Blanketflower
Galeobdolon luteum
    Golden Deadnettle
Gentiana Gentian
Hakonechloa macra 'Aureola'
    Aureola Grass
Hedera Ivy
Hemerocallis (some) Daylily
Herbs
Heuchera Coralbells
Hibiscus mosceutos Rose Mallow
Hosta Plantain Lily
Lamium Dead Nettle
Liatris Gay-feather
Lilium Lily
Lythrum Loosestrife
Miscanthus cvs Silver Grass
Monarda didyma Bee Balm
Oenothera (some)
    Evening Primrose, Sundrops
Origanum vulgare Marjoram
Penstemon Beard-tongue
Phlox subulata Moss Pink
Primula Primrose
Rosmarinus officinalis Rosemary
Scabiosa Pincushion Flower
Sempervivum Hen-and-chickens
Tricyrtis Toad Lily
Verbena canadensis cvs Vervain
Vinca Periwinkle
Viola Pansy, Violet

Perennials adapt well to containers such as patio pots and window-boxes. Most suitable are the low to medium height plants with upright or trailing habit, ones that bloom for a long season so the containers provide attractive displays for as long as possible. In containers, as in the garden, perennials can easily be combined with annuals.

Perennials for container plantings should be those that tolerate rapidly changing water content in well-drained soils. Moisture needs are greatest during hot dry periods when containers frequently need to be watered more than once each day.

Because the volume of soil in containers is relatively small, plant roots are limited for both water and nutrient availability. To keep plants looking their best, a regular feeding program needs to be maintained. Excess salts are likely to build up in the soil during the season, so soil should be replaced when plants are repotted each year.

Lavandula species

Herb Gardens

Perennial herbs form the basis for a complete herb garden that will supply culinary needs and fragrance all year. The best location for such a garden is in an area of good, well-drained soil, part of which is semi-shaded, and which is conveniently accessible from the kitchen.

herbs

The following perennial herbs are described in this book. All are fragrant. Many have culinary value, being used to flavor and enhance foods. Some are used just for their fragrance.

Agastache Hyssop (fragrance)
Allium sativum Garlic
Allium schoenoprasum Chives
Artemisia absinthium
   Common Wormwood (fragrance)
Artemisia dracunculus Tarragon
Artemisia dracunculus var. sativa
   French Tarragon
Calamintha nepeta
Chamaemelum nobile Roman Chamomile
Lavandula angustifolia
   English Lavender (fragrance)
Marrubium vulgare Horehound
Melissa officinalis Lemon Balm
Mentha Mint
Monarda didyma Bee Balm (fragrance)
Nepeta Catmint, Ground Ivy (fragrance)
Origanum vulgare Marjoram
Perovskia atriplicifolia Azure Sage (fragrance)
Rosmarinus officinalis Rosemary
Ruta graveolens Rue (fragrance)
Salvia officinalis Garden Sage
Satureja montana Winter Savory
Thymus Thyme

Natural landscapes

A number of perennials will naturalize among shrubs, wildflowers and bulbs. In fact, many cultivated perennials such as cardinal flower (*Lobelia cardinalis*) and goatsbeard (*Aruncus*) are natives of North America. Natural landscapes, from prairie to woodland, can be planned for low maintenance and seasonal beauty as well as for food and cover for wildlife. Native and naturalized perennials, and perennial wildflowers such as tickseed (*Coreopsis*), that are relatively versatile, are identified in the plant listings. Just as some cultivated perennials find their place in natural plantings, so can these perennial wildflowers be used in more formal settings.

Trillium

ferns

The following ferns are described in this book.

Adiantum pedatum Maidenhair Fern
Athyrium Lady Fern, Japanese Painted Ferns
Dennstaedtia punctiloba Hay-scented Fern
Dryopteris Wood-fern, Shield Ferns
Osmunda Flowering Ferns
Polystichum acrostichoides Christmas Fern

Fern landscape

beds & borders

❧ PERENNIAL BORDERS AND BEDS ❧

Perennials have long been used in carefully thought out flower gardens or in beds that provide beauty, fragrance, and flowers for cutting from spring until late autumn. Good planning helps minimize the maintenance needs of every garden planting. The traditional cottage garden that looks so natural is generally the result of well-planned groupings in which the individual plants neither crowd one another out nor leave unsightly gaps once they have become established.

The traditional position for perennial borders and beds has been at the side or back of the home. Today's gardeners have extended this. While some landscapers reserve the front or public side of a house for a more formal appearance, others are including perennial plantings that add pleasing color and texture where all may enjoy them. For example, an older home, with traditional narrow edgings and borders or foundation plantings of tired evergreens, can be revitalized when these planting spaces are reshaped, widened, or replaced entirely to accommodate colorful plantings that include perennials.

Another goal of today's landscaper and home gardener is to tie the garden to indoor living areas. For this, suitable garden sites are easily viewed from living areas within the home. The beds or borders are not necessar-ily fully visible from indoors: they serve as invitations to come outside where more of the landscape can be seen and enjoyed.

Many variations on the traditional perennial bed or border have appeared in recent years, each one to suit the environment and the homeowners' needs. For example, pockets or groups of tender annuals are planted for seasonal variety. The perennials provide protection and background for the changing annual plantings. In addition, early spring color and attractive accents throughout the year can be achieved by the use of hardy bulbs such as snowdrops (*Galanthus*), crocus, and daffodils (*Narcissus*) among the perennials. And tender plants like lilies find shelter from the heat of summer; they may thrive longer among perennials.

Regardless of the shape a perennial garden takes, it is wise to provide some sort of edging to prevent the encroachment of lawn grasses as well as possible mechanical damage to flowers from lawn equipment. Such an edging will also give the bed form. Bricks, tiles, slates, flagstones, railroad ties, landscape timbers, or plastic lawn edging can be used. Flagstones or decorative masonry blocks are often inserted between plants to provide access for maintenance and cutting.

Borders

Perennial borders have traditionally been long and narrow. Formal landscaping continues the tradition, with variations to suit individual sites and needs. Whatever the length or width of a border, it is usually backed by a building, fence or evergreen screen. This provides a suitable backdrop for the succession of color to come from early spring until autumn. Plants should generally be arranged in stairstep fashion with short plants in front and taller ones at the back. For added visual depth, plant accent groups of taller perennials among lower-growing ones.

When planning a new or renewed perennial border, allow for an access path along the back, behind the tallest plants. A three-foot (90-centimeter) minimum space from the back to the closest plants permits adequate air circulation and the best possible plant growth.

Plants at the back of a border usually need more water than those at the front, not only because they are taller but because of severe competition for soil moisture from shrubs, trees or hedge; a building, wall or fence shelters the back of the border from rain.

Beds

Free-standing perennial beds can be viewed from all sides. They can be any shape: round, oval, square, or the traditional rectangular oblong. For a pleasing all-round appearance, the tallest plants are usually placed in the center, with successively shorter ones towards the perimeter. If an island bed is used as a divider between work and play or leisure areas, the work side might include some plants that are used strictly for cutting, with the main attraction on the side that is seen from the indoor and/or outdoor living areas. The tallest plants in this example might be closer to the work area to allow more variety and depth to be seen from the main viewing area.

flowers for cutting

Perennials that are useful for fresh-cut and/or dried flower or seed-head design (D).

Acanthus mollis Bear's-breech (D)
Achillea Yarrow (D)
Aconitum Monkshood
Alcea rosea Hollyhock
Alchemilla mollis
  Common Lady's-mantle (D)
Anaphalis triplinervis
  Pearly Everlasting (D)
Anemone Windflower
Anthemis Golden Marguerite
Armeria Thrift (D)
Aquilegia Columbine
Artemisia lactiflora White Mugwort
Asclepias tuberosa
  Butterfly Flower (D)
Aster
Astilbe False Spirea (D)
Astrantia major Greater Masterwort
Baptisia australis False Indigo
Belamcanda chinensis
  Blackberry Lily
Bergenia cordifolia
  Heartleaf Bergenia
Boltonia asteroides White Boltonia
Buddleia Butterfly Bush
Campanula (some) Bellflower
Catananche caerulea
  Blue Cupid's-dart (D)
Centaurea Cornflower
Centranthus ruber Red Valerian
Chrysanthemum
Cimicifuga simplex
  Kamchatka Bugbane
Convallaria majalis
  Lily-of-the-valley
Coreopsis Tickseed
Crocosmia Xcrocosmiiflora
  Montbretia
Dahlia
Delphinium
Dianthus
  Pink, Carnation, Sweet William
Dicentra Bleeding-heart
Dictamnus albus Gas Plant (D)
Digitalis Foxglove
Doronicum Leopard's-bane
Echinacea (D)
Echinops Globe Thistle (D)
Erigeron Fleabane
Eryngium Sea Holly
Erysimum cheiri English Wallflower
Eupatorium Boneset
Gaillardia Xgrandiflora
  Blanketflower
Geum Avens

Grasses (D)
Goniolimon tataricum Statice (D)
Gypsophila Baby's-breath (D)
Hedera Ivy (foliage)
Helenium Sneezeweed
Helianthus Sunflower
Heliopsis helianthoides
  Sunflower Heliopsis
Helleborus Christmas/Lenten Rose
Heuchera Coralbells
Hosta Plantain Lily
Incarvillea delavayi Hardy Gloxinia
Inula ensifolia Swordleaf Inula
Iris
Knautia macedonica (D)
Kniphofia uvaria Torch Lily
Lathyrus latifolius Everlasting Pea
Lavandula angustifolia Lavender (D)
Leucanthemum Xsuperbum
  Shasta Daisy
Liatris Gay-feather (D)
Ligularia
Lilium
Limonium latifolium Statice (D)
Lunaria annua Honesty (D)
Lupinus Lupine
Lychnis Campion
Lysimachia (some) Loosestrife
Monarda Wild Bergamot
Paeonia Peony
Papaver nudicaule Iceland Poppy
Perovskia atriplicifolia
  Azure, Russian Sage
Phlox paniculata Garden Phlox
Physalis alkekengi
  Chinese-lantern (D)
Physostegia virginiana
  Obedient Plant
Polemonium caeruleum
  Jacob's-ladder
Polygonatum Solomon's-seal
Primula Primrose
Ranunculus repens
  Creeping Buttercup
Rudbeckia Coneflower
Scabiosa caucasica
  Pincushion Flower
Sidalcea Prairie Mallow
Solidago Goldenrod (D)
XSolidaster luteus
  Hybrid Goldenrod
Stokesia laevis Stoke's Aster
Tanacetum
  Painted Daisy, Matricaria
Thalictrum Meadow Rue
Thermopsis False Lupine
Trollius Globeflower
Veronica (some) Speedwell
Viola Pansy, Violet

Winter months are usually the best time to begin planning any perennial planting. Armchair gardening, with descriptive books, videos, CD-ROMs and catalogs, gives time for reflection and the visualization of an overall scheme with or without detail. Graph paper or a landscaping computer program can be used to plot projected new plantings. When each variety is drawn to scale, the required numbers are easy to determine, Choose varieties that meet needs for color, flowering times, height, spread, and sources of fresh or dried bouquets.

Perennials in groups

Massed perennials have a more pleasing effect when planted in groups rather than rows. Use the spacing recommendations as guides for planting both in groups and in rows (useful in a cutting garden). Even a single plant should be similarly placed so it has adequate air and soil.

Color considerations

Bloom color affects the appearance of any planting. A bed or border that is dominated by bright colors (red, orange, yellow) appears much closer to the viewer than one containing mostly cool tones (blue, gray, green). Whole borders can be designed with one basic tone — gray, for example. Or the combination of bright and cool colors achieves continuing interest as dominant color changes through the growing season.

Buddleia

perennials that attract butterflies

Representatives of these plants are described on pages 25 through 166.

Achillea Yarrow
Alcea Hollyhock
Aquilegia Columbine
Agastache Hyssop
Allium Ornamental Onion
Arabis Rock Cress
Armeria Thrift, Sea Pink
Asclepias Milkweed, Butterfly Flower
Aster
Astilbe False Spirea
Aubrieta Rock Cress
Baptisia Wild or False Indigo
Buddleia Butterfly Bush, Summer Lilac
Caryopteris
Catananche Cupid's-dart
Centaurea Cornflower
Centranthus Valerian
Ceratostigma Leadwort
Chelone Turtlehead
Cimicifuga Bugbane
Coreopsis Tickseed
Delphinium
Dianthus Pink, Carnation
Dictamnus Fraxinella, Dittany
Digitalis Foxglove
Echinacea Coneflower
Echinops Globe Thistle
Erigeron Fleabane
Eryngium amethystinum Sea Holly
Erysimum Wallflower
Eupatorium Boneset
Gaillardia Blanketflower
Hemerocallis Daylily
Hesperis Dame's-rocket, Sweet Rocket
Iberis Candytuft
Lavandula Lavender
Leucanthemum Shasta Daisy
Liatris Blazing-star, Gay-feather
Lobelia Cardinal Flower
Lupinus Lupine
Lythrum Loosestrife
Malva Mallow
Monarda Wild Bergamot
Nepeta Catmint
Origanum Marjoram, Oregano
Penstemon Beard-tongue
Phlox
Physostegia Obedient Plant, False Dragonhead
Potentilla Cinquefoil, Five-finger
Ranunculus Buttercup, Crowfoot
Rudbeckia Coneflower
Salvia Sage, Ramona
Saponaria Soapwort
Scabiosa Pincushion Flower
Sedum Stonecrop, Orpine
Solidago Goldenrod

colorful foliage

SILVERY, BLUE, GRAY-GREEN
Achillea Yarrow
Artemisia Wormwood
Aurinia saxatilis Basket-of-gold
Caryopteris Xclandonensis 'Longwood Blue'
Dianthus spp, cvs Pink, Carnation
Eryngium Sea Holly
Erythronium Dog-tooth Violet
Festuca glauca cvs Blue Fescue
Helictotrichon sempervirens
  Blue Oat Grass
Hosta cvs Plantain Lily
Lamium maculatum cvs
  Spotted Deadnettle
Lavandula Lavender
Leymus arenarius 'Glaucus'
  Lyme Grass
Macleaya cordata Plume poppy
Nepeta Xfassenii
  Persian Ground Ivy
Perovskia atriplicifolia
  Azure Sage, Russian Sage
Pulmonaria saccharata cvs
  Bethlehem Sage
Saccharum ravennae Plume Grass
Salvia cvs Sage
Santolina chamaecyparissus
  Lavender Cotton
Sedum cvs Stonecrop
Stachys byzantina Lamb's-ears
Thymus cvs Thyme
Veronica incana Woolly Speedwell
Yucca Adam's-needle, Soapwort

BRONZE, RED, PURPLE
Ajuga reptans cvs Carpet Bugle
Aster lateriflorus Calico Aster
Astilbe cvs False Spirea
Canna Indian Shot
Euphorbia dulcis 'Cameleon'
  Purple Spurge
Heuchera americana cvs
  American Alumroot
Imperata cylindrica 'Rubra'
  Japanese Blood Grass
Lychnis Xarkwrightii
  Arkwright's Campion
Penstemon digitalis 'Husker Red'
  White Penstemon
Rodgersia aesculifolia
  Fingerleaf Rodgersia
Salvia cvs Sage
Sedum cvs Stonecrop

VARIEGATED
Aegopodium podagraria 'Variegatum'
  Snow-on-the-mountain
Ajania pacifica
  Silver-and-gold Chrysanthemum
Ajuga reptans cvs Carpet Bugle
Cerastium tomentosum
  Snow-in-summer
Carex hachijoensis 'Evergold'
  Silver Variegated Japanese Sedge
Euonymus fortunei cvs
  Wintercreeper
Glyceria maxima 'Variegata'
  Manna Grass
Hakonechloa macra 'Aureola'
Hosta cvs Plantain Lily

Houttuynia cordata
  Chameleon Plant
Iris pallida 'Variegata'
  Variegated Dalmatian Iris
Lamium maculatum cvs
  Spotted Deadnettle
Lirope cvs Lily Turf
Miscanthus sinensis cvs
  Japanese Silver Grass
Molinia caerulea 'Variegata'
  Variegated Moor Grass
Pachysandra terminalis 'Variegata'
  Variegated Japanese Spurge
Phalaris arundinacea cv.
  Ribbon Grass
Sedum cvs Stonecrop
Thymus Variegated Thyme
Vinca cvs Periwinkle
Yucca Adam's-needle, Soapwort

FALL & WINTER COLOR
Bergenia cordifolia
  Heartleaf Bergenia
Ceratostigma plumbaginoides
  Leadwort
Dennstaedtia punctiloba
  Hay-scented Fern
Epimedium cvs Barrenwort
Fallopia Japanese Knotweed
Geranium spp Cranesbill
Persicaria Smartweed
Sedum cvs Stonecrop
Tiarella cordifolia Foamflower

As with most gardening projects, soil preparation for perennials is best begun well ahead of planting time. An early start means that unwanted grassy and broad-leaved weeds can be largely eradicated. Big clumps are best removed by hand during digging. Annual grasses and weeds can be tilled under. Perennial grasses should be removed and destroyed or composted. Fresh weed seedlings, often from seed brought to the surface during soil preparation, are easily killed by hoeing or cultivating in the days and weeks after soil has been prepared. Even small areas, where just a few or only one perennial will be planted, should still be prepared ahead of planting time.

Early preparation — eight weeks ahead of planting would be ideal — is especially important if the soil structure and content need modification. Most perennials like a well-drained soil that is relatively high in organic content and available plant foods. The preferred pH (measure of soil's acidity/alkalinity) is slightly acid to neutral, with pH values of 5.5 to 7.0. Some adjustments may be necessary: these are outlined below.

The soil should be dug or tilled thoroughly to a depth of at least 12 inches (30 centimeters). The deeper it is cultivated, the better the soil will be for perennials. Roots will be able to penetrate more deeply and so withstand drought and cold. A hard pan only 8 to 10 inches (20 to 25 centimeters) down restricts root development. While digging or tilling, add whatever is needed to improve soil structure, pH and nutrients.

Soil structure

To improve a heavy clay soil, work in peat moss, leaves, leaf mold, or other organic matter. If the soil contains a lot of close-knit clay and is fine-textured, gypsum (at 5 pounds per 100 square feet) will help create a more open and friable structure. When drainage is very poor or nonexistent, it may be necessary to lay field drain tile at a depth of 24-36 inches (60-90 centimeters) for the removal of excess water. In a smaller area, bed(s) can be raised with added topsoil to ensure good drainage. For sandy soils, add compost, organic matter, or well-drained topsoil so that sufficient moisture will be retained in the root zone. These modifiers enable soil to provide the air and moisture needed by actively growing roots.

The total quantity of modifier to apply, unless specified otherwise, should be one-third to one-half of the volume of soil to be turned over. In other words, if the ground is to be dug or tilled to the optimum depth of 12" (30cm), use a layer of organic matter 4 to 6 inches (10 to 15 centimeters) deep, spread over the surface before digging begins.

Weedkillers

If chemical weedkillers have been applied, the prepared ground must lie fallow for at least two weeks; follow the recommendations on the product label.

Soil pH and nutrients

Use a soil testing kit or ask the local extension service to measure soil pH and available nutrients.

Add recommended rates of limestone for a change in pH from acid towards neutral. Sulfur or iron sulfate brings an alkaline soil closer to the desired neutral or slightly acidic condition. Add solid garden fertilizer with analysis of about 5-10-5 (low nitrogen, high phosphorus)

Double Digging

Double digging opens up tight soils to a depth of about 20" (50cm). While it is a time-consuming and laborious operation, the long-term result of healthy perennial growth for many years makes double digging worth the effort. During double digging, the subsoil is improved with modifiers, and can either be left under the topsoil (Method A), or be lifted to the surface so the top 20" (50cm) of soil is mixed together (Method B).

Method A	Method B
Subsoil unsuitable for mixing with topsoil (e.g. heavy clay, pure sand, limestone). *Modified subsoil remains below topsoil.*	For soils whose subsoil is similar to topsoil so they can be mixed. *This method lifts modified subsoil to surface.*

STEP 1 (both methods)
Starting at one end or side, remove the top 10" (25cm) of soil from two 12"-wide (30cm) rows; place soil in wheelbarrow or on plastic so it is available to add to the other end or side of the plot. See diagram on opposite page for this and subsequent steps.

STEP 2 Remove and reserve a third 12" (30cm) row of topsoil.	**STEP 2** Dig out lower 10" (25cm) of soil — the subsoil— from first 12" (30cm) row, and set aside for replacing last row of subsoil at the end of the task.
STEP 3 Dig out lower 10" (25cm) of soil — the subsoil— from first 12" (30cm) row, and set aside for replacing last row of subsoil at the end of the task.	**STEP 3** Turn a third topsoil 12" (30cm) row, with modifiers as needed, into the trench left by first row of subsoil.
STEP 4 Spread subsoil modifiers over the surface of second 12" (30cm) row, and turn that row to mix and replace the first.	**STEP 4** Spread subsoil modifiers over the surface of second row, and turn that row onto the top of the first row (topsoil beneath).
STEP 5 Turn fourth 12" (30cm) row of topsoil, with modifiers as needed, onto the top of the mixed subsoil in the first row.	

Repeat last two steps with successive 12"-wide (30cm-wide), 10"-deep (25cm-deep) rows; replace final rows with topsoil and subsoil reserved from first few rows.

See opposite for illustration of double digging (both methods).

at 3-5 pounds per 100 square feet. If undecayed leaves or straw are used as modifiers, also include some high nitrogen ammonium nitrate (2 pounds per 100 square feet) to avoid any sudden loss of nitrogen to the microorganisms that help these "raw" modifiers decay.

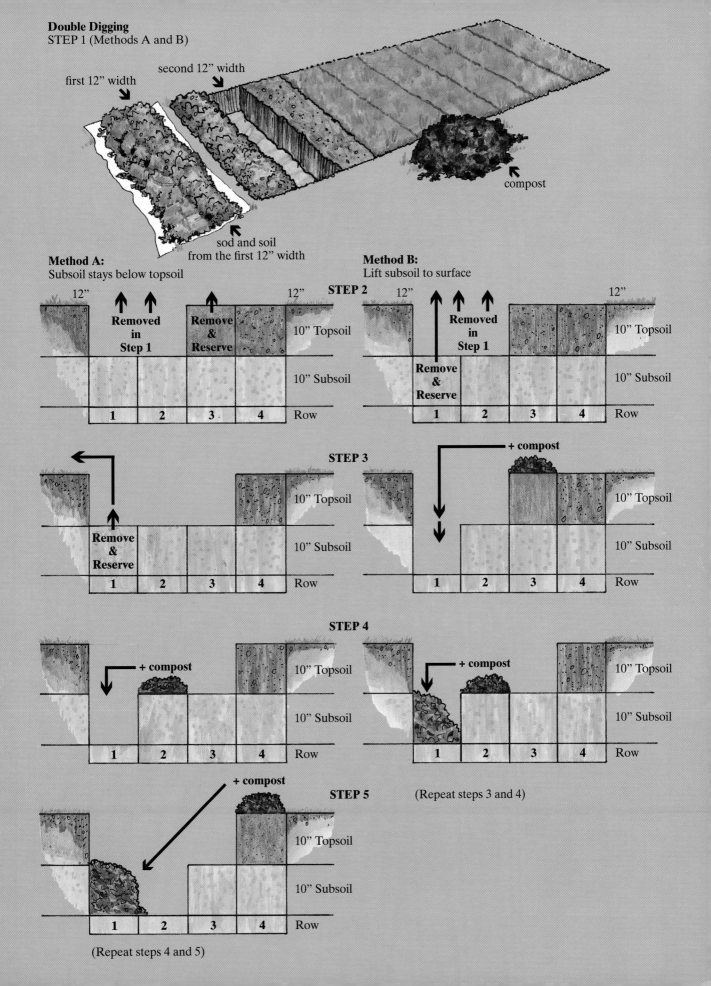

Double Digging
STEP 1 (Methods A and B)

first 12" width

second 12" width

compost

sod and soil
from the first 12" width

Method A:
Subsoil stays below topsoil

Method B:
Lift subsoil to surface

STEP 2

Method A, Step 2:
12"
Removed
in
Step 1
Remove &
Reserve
10" Topsoil
10" Subsoil
1 2 3 4 Row
12"

Method B, Step 2:
12"
Removed
in
Step 1
Remove
&
Reserve
10" Topsoil
10" Subsoil
1 2 3 4 Row
12"

STEP 3

Method A, Step 3:
Remove
&
Reserve
10" Topsoil
10" Subsoil
1 2 3 4 Row

Method B, Step 3:
+ compost
10" Topsoil
10" Subsoil
1 2 3 4 Row

STEP 4

Method A, Step 4:
+ compost
10" Topsoil
10" Subsoil
1 2 3 4 Row

Method B, Step 4:
+ compost
10" Topsoil
10" Subsoil
1 2 3 4 Row

(Repeat steps 3 and 4)

STEP 5

+ compost
10" Topsoil
10" Subsoil
1 2 3 4 Row

(Repeat steps 4 and 5)

Perennial plants are usually available locally from the start of the recommended planting period. Those shipped from a distant nursery should also arrive during the correct season — early to late spring in the North, and fall and spring in southern zones. Plant immediately when possible.

If newly purchased and delivered perennials cannot be planted right away, store them in a cool but not freezing dark place after opening the package tops for aeration. Follow any special directions that come with shipped plants.

Perennials in containers with soil are usually growing or ready-to-grow. Store them for as short a time as possible in a sheltered location with filtered light. Water as needed, once or even twice a day in warm weather.

Bare root perennials: Remove from package and soak roots in water or very dilute fertilizer solution (no more than 25% recommended strength). After 12-24 hours replace soaked plants in waxed/plastic shipping compartments, or lay them in a box of damp peat moss. Repeat in 2-3 days if perennials still cannot be planted. This practice pays off since plants with soaked roots become established more quickly than those whose roots remained dry before planting.

Plant as soon as conditions are good. Set plants on or near their planting positions, still in their pots or plastic bags to prevent drying out. Bare root perennials can be planted direct from their soaking water or solution. Handle plants one at a time so roots have the least exposure to drying air.

Dig holes big enough for the root systems. With one hand support each plant in its hole so that the junction of roots and stem(s) or crown will be at or slightly below the soil surface. With the other hand tumble loose soil around roots and other underground parts. Gently firm soil over or around smaller perennials; larger plants may be tamped or firmed in more securely. Water each newly planted perennial so soil and roots settle in together. In dry conditions, plants are best puddled in with plenty of water, to moisten surrounding soil.

perennials for sun

Many of the following perennials grow well in dry soils. Most can tolerate extreme heat in dry conditions (see next paragraph). Those that require additional water during hot periods (W) or that will tolerate dry soils only in cooler climates (C) are noted here. Heat tolerant plants can withstand prolonged periods (up to 2 months) of full sun with temperatures exceeding 90°F (32°C). These plants survive best in soil that is free of competing roots. A surface mulch helps protect roots from scorching sun and retains as much water as possible.

Acaena microphylla
   New Zealand Bur
Achillea Yarrow
Amsonia tabernaemontana
   Willow Amsonia (C)
Anaphalis triplinervis
   Pearly Everlasting
Anchusa Alkanet, Bugloss
Antennaria Pussy-toes
Anthemis
   Golden Marguerite (W) (C)
Arabis Rock Cress (W) (C)
Armeria maritima Thrift, Sea Pink
Arrhenatherum elatius var. bulbosum
   Tuber Oat Grass (C)
Artemisia Wormwood
Asclepias tuberosa Butterfly Flower
Aurinia saxatilis Basket-of-gold (C)
Baptisia tinctoria Yellow False Indigo
Campanula poscharskyana
   Serbian Bellflower (W)
Catananche Cupid's-dart
Cerastium tomentosum
   Snow-in-summer
Ceratostigma plumbaginoides
   Leadwort
Chamaemelum nobile
   Roman Chamomile
Coreopsis verticillata
   Threadleaf Coreopsis
Coronilla varia Crown Vetch
Cortaderia selloana Pampas Grass
Dianthus Pink, Carnation (W)
Echinacea purpurea
   Purple Coneflower
Echinops Globe Thistle
Elymus arenarius Lyme Grass

Erigeron Fleabane
Eryngium Sea Holly
Euonymus fortunei Wintercreeper
Euphorbia (some) Spurge
Festuca Fescue (W) (C)
Gaillardia Xgrandiflora
   Blanketflower
Geranium (some) Cranesbill
Gypsophila paniculata
   Baby's-breath
Helianthemum Sun Rose
Helictotrichon sempervirens
   Blue Oat Grass
Hemerocallis Daylily
Iris (some)
Kniphofia uvaria Torch Lily
Lavandula angustifolia
   English Lavender
Leontopodium alpinum
   Edelweiss (C)
Leucanthemum Xsuperbum
   Shasta Daisy
Liatris Gay-feather
Linum Flax
Lupinus perennis Wild Lupine
Lychnis viscaria German Catchfly
Malva Mallow
Miscanthus Silver Grass (W) (C)
Nepeta Catmint
Oenothera (most) Sundrops
Penstemon Beard-tongue
Petrorhagia saxifraga Tunic Flower
Phlox subulata Moss Pink
Platycodon grandiflorus
   Balloon Flower
Potentilla Cinquefoil (W)
Rudbeckia Coneflower (W)
Sagina subulata
Salvia Sage
Santolina Lavender Cotton
Saponaria ocymoides
   Rock Soapwort
Sedum Stonecrop
   (not all tolerate heat)
Sempervivum Hen-and-chickens
Solidago Goldenrod
Stachys byzantina Lamb's-ears
Tanacetum parthenium
   Feverfew (W)
Thermopsis False Lupine
Tradescantia Spiderwort
Verbena
Yucca Adam's-needle, Soapwort

1. Dig hole.

2. Position plant in hole.

3. Fill in hole with loose soil. Tamp plant in.

4. Water thoroughly.

perennials for shade

Many partial shade to full shade plants are suitable for planting among trees as well as in other locations shaded by nearby buildings or walls. These perennials are grouped by soil moisture preference and tolerance: extra-moist, moderate/consistent moisture available, and dry conditions The notation (S) denotes plants that grow deep shade.

Shade — extra-moist to wet soil
Adiantum pedatum
  Maidenhair Fern (S)
Alchemilla erythropoda
  Dwarf Lady's-mantle (S)
Alchemilla mollis Lady's-mantle
Athyrium Lady Fern (S)
Brunnera macrophylla
  Heartleaf Brunnera (S)
Cimicifuga Bugbane (S)
Convallaria majalis
  Lily-of-the-valley (S)
Deschampsia caespitosa
  Tufted Hair Grass (S)
Epimedium Barrenwort (S)
Erythronium Dog-tooth Violet
Hosta Plantain Lily (S)
Houttuynia cordata
  Chameleon Plant (S)
Mertensia virginica
  Virginia Bluebells (S)
Osmunda Flowering Ferns (S)
Polygonatum Solomon's-seal (S)
Polystichum acrostichoides
  Christmas Fern (S)
Tiarella False Miterwort (S)
Tricyrtis Toad Lily (S)
Trillium Wake-robin (S)

Shade — moderate, consistent moisture
Acanthus mollis Bear's-breech
Aconitum Monkshood
Adenophora Ladybells
Aegopodium Bishop's Weed (S)
Ajuga Bugleweed
Amsonia tabernaemontana
  Blue Star Flower
Anemone Windflower
Aquilegia Columbine

Arenaria Sandwort
Arisaema triphyllum
  Jack-in-the-pulpit (S)
Arrhenatherum elatius var. bulbosum
  Tuber Oat Grass
Artemisia lactiflora White Mugwort
Aruncus Goatsbeard
Asarum Wild Ginger (S)
Astilbe False Spirea
Astrantia major
  Greater Masterwort (S)
Belamcanda chinensis
  Blackberry Lily
Campanula Bellflower
Chelone lyonii Turtlehead
Chrysogonum virginianum
  Goldenstar (S)
Clematis terniflora
  Sweet Autumn Clematis
Corydalis lutea Yellow Corydalis (S)
Dennstaedtia punctiloba
  Hay-scented Fern (S)
Dicentra Bleeding-heart
Digitalis Foxglove
Dryopteris
  Wood-fern, Shield Ferns (S)
Euonymus fortunei
  Wintercreeper (S)
Ferns
Filipendula Meadowsweet
Galium odoratum Sweet Woodruff
Gaura lindheimeri White Gaura
Gentiana acaulis Stemless Gentian
Hakonechloa macra 'Aureola'
  Aureola Grass
Hedera helix English Ivy (S)
Helleborus
  Christmas/Lenten Rose (S)
Heuchera Coralbells
Imperata cylindrica 'Rubra'
  Japanese Blood Grass
Iris (some)
Lamium Deadnettle (S)
Lamium galeobdolon
  Golden Deadnettle (S)
Lunaria annua Money Plant
Lysimachia punctata
  Yellow Loosestrife
Monarda Wild Bergamot
Myosotis sylvatica
  Woodland Forget-me-not

Pachysandra terminalis
  Japanese Spurge (S)
Papaver nudicaule Iceland Poppy
Phlox divaricata Wild Blue Phlox
Polemonium Jacob's-ladder
Primula Primrose
  (moist soil esp. in hot regions)
Pulmonaria Lungwort
Pulsatilla vulgaris
  European Pasqueflower
Ranunculus repens
  Creeping Buttercup
Rodgersia aesculifolia
  Fingerleaf Rodgersia
Sanguinaria canadensis Bloodroot
Symphytum caucasicum
  Blue Comfrey
Thalictrum Meadow Rue
Tradescantia Spiderwort
Trollius Globeflower
Vinca Periwinkle (S)
Viola Pansy, Violet
Waldsteinia Barren Strawberry (S)

Shade —dry soil
Dry shade is one of the most challenging of gardening conditions. Not only is sunlight lacking, but soil moisture is depleted by nearby trees, shrubs or structures. The soil itself may be poor and dusty. Added organic matter improves soil; regular watering and fertilizing help supply plant needs.

Adonis amurensis Amur Adonis
Anaphalis triplinervis
  Pearly Everlasting
Euonymus fortunei Wintercreeper
Geranium sanguineum Cranesbill
Lamium maculatum
  Spotted Deadnettle (S)
Liriope Lilyturf
Pachysandra terminalis
  Japanese Spurge (S)
Pulmonaria saccharata
  Bethlehem Sage
Sagina subulata
  Corsican Pearlwort (S)
Stachys byzantina Lamb's-ears
Symphytum grandiflorum
  Large-flowered Comfrey
Vinca Periwinkle (S)

Watering and Fertilizing

The need to water perennials varies from place to place as well as from month to month. Where watering is needed much of the time, a more or less permanent system of soaker hoses lying on the ground would be best.

Newly planted perennials usually need added fertilizer once or twice during the first growing season. Make one early summer application of a granular 5-10-5 formulation at 2 pounds per 100 square feet (975 grams per 10 square meters), or use liquid fertilizer. Apply liquids at half the recommended rate to avoid burning tender young shoots and supplying too much nitrogen which leads to excess leafy growth. A second application can be made six weeks later.

For established perennial plantings, surface or liquid applications of an all-round garden fertilizer two or three times during the year will provide adequate amounts of plant food. One application should be in early spring while plants are still dormant, another six weeks into the growing season, and the third in mid to late summer.

Foliar sprays of dilute liquid fertilizer will bring almost immediate though short-term results. For the best results when plants show signs of nutrient deficiencies, combine foliar feeding with soil applications. A regular fertilization program, though, should ensure healthy plant growth and development.

Weed Control

While perennials are small it's an easy task to hand-weed or hoe lightly between the plants to prevent weeds from becoming established and from competing with the perennials for moisture and nutrients. As perennials grow and spread, weeds will be fewer. Remove those that do grow so the perennials can continue their unrestricted development. Add mulch to the weed-free soil between (but not touching) perennials for further weed control.

Mulching

Mulches control weeds, conserve moisture, and protect plant roots from temperature extremes. Decaying organic mulches also modify the soil; however, extra nitrogen fertilizer may be needed as the mulch breaks down (see page 12). Spread mulch between plants, taking care to avoid burying or crowding tender shoots.

A spring application of shredded bark, peat moss, leaves or other material will reduce weed growth and water losses. Most perennials also perform better in spring after a late fall application of straw, leaves or small evergreen branches to protect against winter damage. The need for winter protection is greatest when perennials are planted at the northern limits of their hardiness zones. Both hardiness and heat zone ratings are included for each group of perennials on pages 25-166. The USDA hardiness zone map, on the inside front cover, helps gardeners determine which perennials will live through winters in their locales.

Staking/Support

Taller-growing perennials such as some varieties of aster need support to prevent their flopping over. While the plants are still fairly short (and before they start to fall), insert branching twigs among the foliage and between plants. Subsequent growth will cover the twigs. For the individual heavy stems of, say, delphinium or hollyhock (*Alcea rosea*), use single canes, stakes, or other supports. More than one tie per stem will be needed as the plant grows.

Trimming

Dead-heading (removal of dead flowers) and trimming off damaged parts during the growing season will maintain neat, trim, long-blooming perennials.

Fall Cleanup, Winter

When top growth has died back, trim for neatness as desired. Clean out weeds before they become established. Remove old growth entirely to reduce overwintering fungus and insects. However, in northern zones leave some top growth for protection. If tops must be trimmed back, apply winter mulch after the ground has frozen to protect against alternate thawing and freezing which tends to lift plants out of the soil. In early spring, remove the mulch and any remaining dead plant parts.

Perennials may also be divided in fall, especially where winters are not severe; the newly planted sections will develop new roots before winter. If freezing weather is close at hand, plan to divide plants in early spring.

Plant Zones

Plant zones are guides to a plant's ability to grow well in a given location with normal, average expected extremes of cold and heat. Hardiness and heat zone maps show where each plant can be expected to thrive.

Hardiness zones indicate how much cold a plant can withstand while continuing to grow normally. The eleven hardiness zones are based on average annual minimum temperatures, from the coldest, zone 1 with winter temperatures of -50°F (-45°C) and colder, to the warmest, zone 11 where winters are warmer than 40°F (5°C).

Heat zones are guides to a plant's heat tolerance. They are based on the average number of days during which the temperature can normally be expected to rise higher than 86°F (30°C). This is the temperature at which plant cell proteins begin to be damaged. The twelve heat zones range from the hottest, 12, with more than 210 days of potentially damaging heat, to the coolest, zone 1 in which the temperature may reach 86°F (30°C) for an average of less than one day per year.

Hardiness zones are stated from lower to higher number, coldest to warmest winter temperatures. Heat zones are stated from hottest to coolest so the larger number appears first. In plant descriptions, hardiness zones are usually placed before heat zones.

Plants may survive more extremes of heat and cold than indicated by zone designations, but growth will be marginal and often less than ideal. However, just about every garden, even the smallest, has variations in both lowest and highest temperatures. Make use of microclimates that result from the influences of topography, landscape, building(s) and cultural practices. Less hardy plants thrive in sheltered corners, protected southern or western aspects, or with extra care to help them through the coldest times. Use tougher, hardier items in exposed areas. Permanent shade and/or nearby water features reduce extreme heat for plants that otherwise might quickly fade away and die.

moisture tolerant perennials

These plants will grow in extra-moist or boggy soils; most of them also thrive in moderately moist conditions.

Aconitum Monkshood
Aegopodium Bishop's Weed
Arenaria montana
　Mountain Sandwort
Arisaema triphyllum
　Jack-in-the-pulpit
Aruncus Goatsbeard
Asarum Wild Ginger
Asclepias incarnata Swamp Milkweed
Astilbe False Spirea
Athyrium Lady Fern
Baptisia australis Blue False Indigo
Bergenia cordifolia
　Heartleaf Bergenia
Boltonia asteroides White Boltonia
Brunnera macrophylla
　Heartleaf Brunnera
Calamagrostis Reed Grass
Caltha palustris Marsh Marigold (B)
Campanula Bellflower
Chelone lyonii Turtlehead
Cimicifuga Bugbane
Coreopsis rosea Rose Coreopsis
Deschampsia caespitosa
　Tufted Hair Grass (B)
Digitalis Foxglove

Epimedium Barrenwort
Eupatorium (some) Boneset
Euphorbia griffithii Griffith's Spurge
Fallopia japonica var. compacta
　Magic Carpet (B)
Filipendula Meadowsweet (B)
Galium odoratum Sweet Woodruff
Geranium sanguineum
　Blood-red Cranesbill
Glyceria maxima 'Variegata'
　Manna Grass
Helenium Sneezeweed
Hemerocallis Daylily
Hosta Plantain Lily
Houttuynia cordata
　Chameleon Plant (B)
Iberis Candytuft
Inula ensifolia Swordleaf Inula
Iris ensata Japanese Iris (B)
Iris sibirica Siberian Iris (B)
Iris versicolor Wild Iris (B)
Liatris Gay-feather
Ligularia
Liriope Lilyturf
Lobelia siphilitica
　Blue Cardinal Flower (B)
Lysimachia Loosestrife
Mentha Mint
Mertensia virginica
　Virginia Bluebells
Molinia caerulea Purple Moor Grass

Monarda Wild Bergamot
Myosotis scorpioides
　Water Forget-me-not (B)
Nepeta Catmint
Osmunda claytoniana
　Interrupted Fern
Paeonia suffruticosa Tree Peony
Persicaria Smartweed, Knotweed
Phalaris arundinacea var. picta
　Ribbon Grass
Phlox (some)
Physostegia virginiana
　Obedient Plant
Polemonium Jacob's-ladder
Polygonatum Solomon's-seal
Polygonum Knotweed
Primula japonica
　Japanese Primrose (B)
Pulmonaria Lungwort
Ranunculus repens
　Creeping Buttercup
Rodgersia aesculifolia
　Fingerleaf Rodgersia (B)
Sanguinaria canadensis Bloodroot
Sanguisorba Burnet (B)
Symphytum Comfrey
Thalictrum Meadow Rue
Tiarella False Miterwort
Tradescantia Spiderwort
Trillium Wake-robin
Trollius Globeflower (B)

Groundcover plants come from four major plant groups: shrubs, conifers, woody vines, and perennials. Each group provides similar benefits of landscape feature as well as erosion control, protection of more tender plants, and modification of the environment. Perennial groundcovers are versatile and are especially useful where quick cover is needed.

Perennial alternatives to turfgrass

Grass is the most familiar groundcover for tying together landscape elements (trees and shrubs, buildings, fences, paved areas). Conservation-wise and for low-maintenance gardening, alternative groundcover plants can be utilized in locations other than high traffic and play areas. And where grass may be impractical from either a maintenance or a visual standpoint, other perennial groundcover plants can be used to greater advantage.

Hedera helix

Houttuynia cordata 'Chameleon'

For example, on a steep embankment which is nearly impossible to mow, a cover of moss phlox (*Phlox subulata*) or periwinkle (*Vinca*) provides a welcome alternative to grass. In a shaded area, spreading bugleweeds (*Ajuga*) or silveredge bishop's-weed (*Aegopodium podograria* 'Variegatum') can replace weak grass. The sun-loving evergreen candytuft (*Iberis sempervirens*) and stonecrop (*Sedum*) thrive in conditions that could burn out regular grass. And creeping Jenny (*Lysimachia nummularia*) does better than grass in damp areas.

Perennials in other areas

Some parts of the landscape naturally suit non-grass groundcovers. One example is the slim strip of soil between house and path or driveway. Another narrow area is near the foundation, between shrubs or conifers. A perennial groundcover (other than turfgrass) planted beneath a fence softens the stark lines of the fence, and the homeowner does not have the repetitive chore of handtrimming grass around fenceposts.

Erosion control

Groundcover plants prevent soil erosion in two ways. First, those with dense branching growth such as lavender cotton (*Santolina*) reduce the force of raindrops by breaking up each drop into smaller droplets that, rather than bounce or run off the soil surface, soak in gradually. Second, a number of perennial groundcovers root from rapidly spreading stems or stolons, binding the soil so it is less likely to be blown or washed away.

English ivy (*Hedera helix*), spring cinquefoil (*Potentilla tabernaemontana*), and mother-of-thyme (*Thymus serpyllum*) are ideal for embankment plantings. If the slope is too great for soil to hold before the new planting has become established, use temporary or permanent artificial stabilizers such as rock or wood terraces, installed across the slope.

Protection against mechanical damage

Perennial groundcovers can also act as protective barriers for trees and shrubs that are likely to be damaged by lawnmowers. An edging of lavender cotton (*Santolina*), for example, eliminates the need to mow, sweep, or spread close to these permanent landscape plantings.

Healthy microclimate

Groundcover plants serve to modify the environment for neighboring plants: low-growing perennials such as lily-of-the-valley (*Convallaria*) and periwinkle (*Vinca*), teamed with clematis vines or rhododendron, provide the shade and moisture necessary to keep roots cool — essential for the growth of these shallow-rooted plants. In the same way, groundcovers cool the home environment. When sunbaked areas around the house are planted with drought tolerant groundcovers such as stonecrop (*Sedum*), soil surface temperatures are reduced. Plant transpiration also helps cool the atmosphere.

Phlox subulata in bloom, with *Sedum*

groundcover perennials

Acaena microphylla
New Zealand Bur
Achillea tomentosa Woolly Yarrow
Aegopodium Bishop's Weed
Aethionema Stonecress
Ajania pacifica
Silver-and-gold Chrysanthemum
Ajuga Bugleweed
Alchemilla (some) Lady's-mantle
Anacyclus pyrethrum var. depressus
Mount Atlas Daisy
Antennaria Pussy-toes
Arabis Rock Cress
Arenaria Sandwort
Armeria maritima Thrift, Sea Pink
Artemisia schmidtiana
Silver Mound Artemisia
Asarum Wild Ginger
Aster lateriflorus Calico Aster
Aubrieta deltoidea
Purple Rock Cress
Aurinia saxatilis Basket-of-gold
Bergenia cordifolia
Heartleaf Bergenia
Brunnera macrophylla
Heartleaf Brunnera
Campanula (some) Bellflower
Cerastium tomentosum
Snow-in-summer
Ceratostigma plumbaginoides
Leadwort
Chamaemelum nobile
Roman Chamomile
Chrysogonum virginianum
Goldenstar
Clematis (some)
Convallaria majalis Lily-of-the-valley

Coronilla varia Crown Vetch
Dianthus (some) Pink
Dicentra (some) Bleeding-heart
Duchesnea indica Mock Strawberry
Epimedium Barrenwort
Euonymus fortunei 'Colorata'
Purpleleaf Wintercreeper
Ferns
Fragaria
Strawberry, ornamental & fruiting
Galium odoratum Sweet Woodruff
Geranium (some) Cranesbill
Grasses (some)
Gypsophila repens
Creeping Baby's-breath
Hedera Ivy
Helianthemum nummularium
Common Sun Rose
Hemerocallis Daylilies
Herniaria glabra Herniary
Heuchera Alumroot, Coral Bells
Hosta Plantain Lily
Houttuynia cordata
Chameleon Plant
Hypericum calycinum
St. John's Wort
Iberis Candytuft
Inula ensifolia Swordleaf Inula
Lamium Dead Nettle
Lamium galeobdolon
Golden Deadnettle
Lathyrus latifolius Everlasting Pea
Liriope Lilyturf
Lysimachia nummularia
Creeping Jenny
Mentha pulegium Pennyroyal
Nepeta Catmint
Nierembergia repens Cupflower

Oenothera
Evening Primrose, Sundrops
Pachysandra terminalis
Japanese Spurge
Papaver nudicaule Iceland Poppy
Persicaria Smartweed, Knotweed
Petrorhagia saxifraga Tunic Flower
Phlox (some)
Polemonium reptans
Creeping Jacob's-ladder
Polygonum aubertii
Silver Fleece Vine
Potentilla neumanniana
Spring Cinquefoil
Primula japonica Japanese Primrose
Pulmonaria Lungwort
Ranunculus repens
Creeping Buttercup
Sagina subulata Corsican Pearlwort
Sanguinaria canadensis Bloodroot
Santolina Lavender Cotton
Saponaria ocymoides Rock Soapwort
Sedum Stonecrop
Sempervivum
Houseleek, Hen-and-chickens
Stachys byzantina Lamb's-ears
Symphytum grandiflorum
Large-flowered Comfrey
Teucrium chamaedrys 'Prostratum'
Germander
Thymus Thyme
Tiarella False Miterwort
Tradescantia virginiana Spiderwort
Verbena canadensis Vervain
Veronica Speedwell
Vinca Periwinkle
Viola odorata Sweet Violet
Waldsteinia Barren Strawberry

The rock garden has long been a favorite way to display low-growing perennials and herbs. Not only can it make use of an otherwise little used hillside location, but, when skillfully constructed, it gives the appearance of a natural rocky outcrop. Even a relatively flat area may be built up with soil and rocks to provide the necessary well-drained, stony conditions.

The most attractive rock garden perennials are those that grow to a height of 12-15 inches (30-38 cm). Some are upright growers, others form clumps, and many creep or trail. The specialty group of Alpines originated above 3,200 feet in mountainous areas of the world; these and other suitable perennials share a need for well-drained soils and full sun. To meet this need, rock gardens should not be shaded; plants should be far enough away from shrubs or trees to avoid competition for available light and moisture. Position plants in a hilly rock garden according to their light and moisture needs, keeping those that grow best in dry conditions near the top of the slope.

Ajania pacifica

rock garden perennials

The following list is a selection of perennials for rock gardens of all sizes, as well as the fronts of borders and in raised beds.

Acaena microphylla
New Zealand Bur
Adonis Amur Adonis
Aethionema Stonecress
Ajania pacifica
Silver-and-Gold Chrysanthemum
Ajuga genevensis
Geneva Bugleweed
Anacyclus Mount Atlas Daisy
Anemone blanda Windflower
Antennaria Pussy-toes
Anthemis marschalliana
Marshall Chamomile
Aquilegia flabellata Fan Columbine
Arabis Rock Cress
Arenaria Sandwort
Armeria maritima Thrift, Sea Pink
Aruncus aethusifolius
Miniature Goatsbeard
Aster alpinus Alpine Aster
Aubrieta deltoidea
Purple Rock Cress
Aurinia saxatilis Basket-of-gold
Bellis perennis English Daisy
Bergenia cordifolia
Heartleaf Bergenia
Campanula (some) Bellflower
Centranthus Valerian
Cerastium tomentosum
Snow-in-summer

Ceratostigma plumbaginoides
Leadwort
Chrysogonum virginianum
Green-and-gold
Coreopsis, smaller forms
Corydalis lutea Yellow Corydalis
Dianthus
Pink, Carnation, Sweet William
Dicentra Bleeding-heart
Erigeron Fleabane
Erysimum cheiri English Wallflower
Euonymus fortunei Wintercreeper
Euphorbia myrsinites
Myrtle Euphorbia
Festuca glauca Blue fescue
Fragaria
Strawberry, ornamental & fruiting
Gentiana Gentian
Geranium Cranesbill
Geum Xborisii Boris Avens
Gypsophila repens
Creeping Baby's-breath
Helianthemum Sun Rose
Helictotrichon Oat Grass
Hemerocallis Daylily
Herniaria glabra Herniary
Heuchera Coralbells
Hosta Plantain Lily
Hypericum calycinum
St. John's Wort
Iberis Candytuft
Incarvillea delavayi Hardy Gloxinia
Inula ensifolia Swordleaf Inula
Iris (some)
Leontopodium alpinum Edelweiss
Linum Flax

Liriope spp & cvs Lilyturf
Lysimachia nummularia
Creeping Jenny
Myosotis alpestris
Alpine Forget-me-not
Nepeta Xfaassenii
Persian Ground Ivy
Nierembergia repens Cupflower
Papaver burseri Alpine Poppy
Papaver nudicaule Iceland Poppy
Pennisetum Fountain Grass
Penstemon (small forms)
Beard-tongue
Petrorhagia saxifraga Tunic Flower
Phlox stolonifera Creeping Phlox
Phlox subulata Moss Phlox
Platycodon grandiflorus var. mariesii
Dwarf Balloon Flower
Potentilla Cinquefoil
Primula Primrose
Pulsatilla vulgaris
European Pasqueflower
Sagina subulata Corsican Pearlwort
Salvia spp & cvs Sage
Santolina Lavender Cotton
Saponaria Soapwort
Sedum Stonecrop
Sempervivum Hen-and-chickens
Stachys byzantina Lamb's-ears
Thymus Thyme
Tiarella sp. Wherry's Foamflower
Tricyrtis Toad Lily
Verbena Vervain
Veronica Speedwell
Vinca Periwinkle
Viola Violet

Basics for rock garden construction

- Start building at the bottom.
- Use larger rocks first so upper rockery is supported. Cement may be needed for added stability.
- Tilt flatter rocks and slabs into the slope to catch moisture and to channel it towards plant roots.
- Fill in with soil and smaller rocks/stones.
- When completed, about two-thirds of each rock's volume will be covered with soil and/or adjacent rocks.

Retaining walls

Rock walls sometimes are built to support steeply sloping banks or as part of a garden terracing project. Leaning into the slope, these mortarless walls will last for many years. Creeping and trailing rock garden plants, set into pockets between the stones, add beauty and help stabilize embankment soil.

Cerastium tomentosum

perennials that attract hummingbirds

A feature common to flowers that attract hummingbirds is a relatively long tube of petals. Flowers are often colorful too. The plants listed here are described in this book.

Alcea Hollyhock
Aquilegia Columbine
Asclepias Milkweed
Campanula Bellflower
Clematis Virgin's-bower
Crocosmia Montbretia
Delphinium
Dianthus Pink, Carnation
Digitalis Foxglove
Echinops Globe Thistle
Hemerocallis Daylily
Heuchera Alumroot
Hibiscus Rose Mallow
Iris Flag, Fleur-de-lis
Kniphofia
    Torch Lily, Poker Plant, Tritoma
Lobelia Cardinal Flower
Lupinus Lupine
Lychnis Campion, Catchfly
Lythrum Loosestrife
Monarda
    Wild Bergamot, Horsemint
Nepeta Catmint
Papaver Poppy
Penstemon Beard-tongue
Phlox paniculata Garden Phlox
Physostegia
    Obedient Plant, False Dragonhead
Salvia Sage, Ramona
Saponaria Soapwort
Veronica Speedwell, Brooklime

ornamental grasses

THE ORNAMENTAL GRASSES

Ornamental grasses are useful in home and commercial landscapes because of their relatively low maintenance and interesting foliage that contrasts well with that of shrubs and flowering perennials. Heights range from less than 12" (30cm) to varieties growing 10' (3m) or more. A number of these grasses are extremely hardy, providing year round displays. Most should be planted in well-drained soils, and mulched during winter in the north to help assure vigorous growth the following spring. Taller varieties should be cut back in early spring to encourage new growth and for a fresh appearance.

Today's uses for ornamental grasses are little different from those of Far Eastern gardeners in earlier times. Low-growing clump or mound styles are useful as bed edging, accents in rock gardens or as groundcover. Blue fescue (*Festuca ovina* var. *glauca*), with its compact habit and stiff grassy blades radiating from the base, forms dense mounds. Tuber oat grass (*Arrhenatherum elatius* var. *bulbosum*) is similar with softer, cascading variegated foliage and a tolerance of shade. Taller clumps are formed by rose fountain grass (*Pennisetum alopecuroides*), whose ornamental fluffy plumes of silvery rose flowers are borne from mid to late summer. This grass makes a good accent plant. And its flowers, like those of other plume-forming grasses, can be cut for drying and arranging.

Medium height ornamental grasses may be planted near the back of a border, perhaps accompanying shrubs. They are often used in dried arrangements. Maiden grass (*Miscanthus sinensis* 'Gracillimus') produces rich green foliage and tall spikes of feathery fine textured creamy white flowers; if left in the garden over winter, foliage and plumes turn an attractive golden color. Another in this group is variegated fountain grass (*M. sinensis* 'Zebrinus'), spectacular with its gold and green striped leaves and feathery pink and beige plumes; this one tolerates some shade and does well in damp locations, making it valuable near ponds or in low areas of the garden.

The taller ornamental grasses are often used singly as specimens in the landscape, or with several clumps making an effective screen. They provide good backgrounds for shorter flowering plants. One of the tallest is pampas grass (*Cortaderia selloana*), which grows to a height of 8-12' (2.4-3.6m). This narrow-leafed grass produces large plumes of creamy white or rose flowers in September and October. While reliably hardy only in zones 6 or 7 through 10, it will survive in portions of more northerly zones. The hardier plume grass (*Erianthus ravennae*) is reliable to zone 5 and grows at least as tall as pampas grass.

grasses and grass-like perennials

The following grasses and grass-like perennials are described in this book.

Arrhenatherum elatius var. bulbosum Tuber Oat Grass
Calamagrostis Reed Grass
Carex hachijoensis 'Evergold'
   Variegated Japanese Sedge
Cortaderia selloana Pampas Grass
Deschampsia caespitosa Tufted Hair Grass
Dianthus Pink, Carnation
Festuca Fescue
Glyceria maxima 'Variegata' Manna Grass, Sweet Grass
Hakonechloa macra 'Aureola' Aureola Grass
Helictotrichon sempervirens Blue Oat Grass, Avena
Imperata cylindrica 'Rubra' Japanese Blood Grass
Leymus arenarius 'Glaucus' Lyme Grass
Liriope Lilyturf
Miscanthus Silver Grass
Molinia caerulea Purple Moor Grass
Panicum virgatum Switch Grass
Pennisetum alopecuroides Fountain Grass
Petrorhagia saxifraga Tunic Flower, Coat Flower
Phalaris arundinacea var. picta Ribbon Grass
Saccharum ravennae Ravenna Grass, Plume Grass
Tradescantia virginiana Spiderwort

plant descriptions

❧ GUIDE TO PERENNIALS - PLANT DESCRIPTIONS ❧

The perennials described on the following pages are arranged alphabetically by botanical name. The common name or names are given with each entry. For quick reference, all these names (both common and botanical) can be found in the index to plant names on pages 167 through 176.

Every genus or group of plants is illustrated with at least one full color photograph. In order to include as many good perennial subjects as possible, some detailed cultivar listings have been restricted to those that are most readily available.

Each plant description includes one or more symbols for speedy recognition of the perennial's light requirements and other specific details.

☼ = Full Sun

⛅ = Partial Shade, Partial Sun
    or sun for part of the day

☁ = Shade, no direct sun

〰 = Groundcover plant

✂ = Cut Flowers, fresh or dried

🌲 = Evergreen plant
    in most climates

🦋 = attracts Butterflies

🐦 = attracts Hummingbirds

Acaena microphylla

Acanthus mollis

ACAENA (a-SEE-na) ☼ ♣
A. microphylla (my-kroh-FIL-a)
New Zealand Bur
Low growing evergreen with bronze-green foliage;
mounds 2-4" (5-10cm). Moist or dry soil. Good in rock
gardens. Inconspicuous late summer flowers are fol-
lowed by colorful red-spiny fruits (burs). Give winter
protection in northern zones. Spreading, rooting stems.
Zones: 6-9, heat 8-6
Spacing: 9-15" (23-38cm)
Propagation: division in spring, seed in fall

A trickle irrigation system reduces water use and
lowers the disease-spreading potential of overhead
sprinklers. Compared with hand-watering, trickle irrigation saves time. The slower application can also
provide better coverage and penetration.

ACANTHUS (a-KAN-thus) ☼ ☁ ♣
Elegant, stately border plants with deeply cut foliage
that mounds 3-4' (0.9-1.2m) high. Spires of bicolored
flowers rise above leaves. Best in well-drained soil.
Semi-evergreen in southern zones. Long-lived perennial
spreads steadily once established.
Zones: 6-9, heat 12-1
Spacing: 24-36" (60-90cm)
Propagation: seed, root cuttings, division

A. mollis (MOL-is)
Bear's-breeches
White and lilac colored flowers on 18" (45cm) erect
spikes open in late spring and early summer.

A. spinosus 'Spinosissimus'
Hybrid bear's-breeches with spinier, often more deeply
divided foliage.

Achillea 'Terra Cotta'

ACHILLEA (a-KIL-ee-a) ☼ ✂ 🦷
Yarrow

Easy to grow, drought-tolerant plants. Best in well-drained soil. Shorter varieties good for rock gardens and foreground, taller ones rarely need support in middle and background plantings. Fern-like foliage has pungent odor. Flowers usually small but numerous, in flat-topped or rounded clusters; excellent for dried arrangements.
Zones: 3-9, heat 9-2
Spacing: 12-24" (30-60cm): see individual species
Propagation: division in spring or fall, seed (species), root cuttings

A. 'Anthea': luminous, pale yellow flowers on 24-36" (60-90cm) stems. Silvery foliage in well-defined mound. Long flowering season, summer to fall. Space 18-24" (45-60cm).

A. 'Coronation Gold': gray-green foliage. Mounds 30-36" (75-90cm). Flowers for long period from late spring to summer; flat, mustard-yellow clusters 3-4" (8-10cm) across. Cut flowers dry well. Space 24-30" (60-75cm).

A. 'Credo': soft yellow flower clusters on green stems. Green to gray-green foliage. Grows 30-36" (75-90cm) high. Excellent to cut for dried arrangements. Space 24" (60cm).

A. 'Moonshine': deeply cut, silvery-gray foliage. Sulfur-yellow flowers in summer on 24" (60cm) plants. Provide excellent drainage for best results. Space 12" (30cm).

A. 'Terra Cotta': multicolored effect as flowers change gradually from peach to clay pot color. Grows 30-36" (75-90cm) tall. Space 15" (38cm).

A. Galaxy Hybrids
Larger flowers and stronger stems resulted from a cross between *A. millefolium* and *A. taygetea*. Foliage similar to that of *A. millefolium*. Height to 36" (90cm). Space 12-18" (30-45cm).

'Appleblossom': clear peach-pink flowers.
'Beacon': crimson-red blossoms have yellow centers.
'Great Expectations': sandstone yellow flowers, 24" (60cm) high.
'Salmon Beauty': large, light salmon-pink flowers.

A. filipendulina (fi-li-pen-dew-LEE-na)
Fern-leaf Yarrow
Mounds 3-5' (0.9-1.5m). Foliage deep-cut, feathery. Summer flowers; flat, yellow clusters 5" (13cm) across. Space 30-36" (75-90cm).
'Gold Plate': deep yellow; height to 5' (1.5m).
'Parker's Variety': golden yellow; height 3-4' (0.9-1.2m).

A. millefolium (mil-ee-FOH-li-um)
Common Yarrow
Rapid spreader with mat-like habit, 12-24" (30-60cm) tall. Dark green, deeply cut foliage. Flowers from midsummer to early fall; colors vary white to red, larger individual florets than those of yellow-flowered yarrows. Naturalized. Space 36" (90cm).
'Paprika': ruby-red; height to 24" (60cm).
'Rosea': rose-pink; height to 20" (50cm).
'Red Beauty': crimson-red; height to 18" (45cm).

A. ptarmica (TAR-mi-ka)
Sneezewort
Vigorously spreading plant, 12-24" (30-60cm) high. Dark green willow-like finely-toothed leaves. White, ball-shaped flower clusters in summer. Naturalized. Space 12-15" (30-38cm). Hardy to zone 2.

A. tomentosa (toh-men-TOH-sa) 〰
Woolly Yarrow
Low-growing spreader mounds 6-12" (15-30cm) high. Good rock garden plant. Grows vigorously in ideal conditions. Light grayish-green, hairy foliage. Sulfur-yellow flowers in early summer; cut flowers dry well. Naturalized. Space 12-15" (30-38cm). Zones 3-7.

Achillea 'Coronation Gold'

Achillea 'Credo'

Achillea 'Moonshine'

Achillea millefolium

Achillea ptarmica

Achillea tomentosa

ACONITUM (a-ko-NY-tum) ☀ ☁ ✄
Monkshood
Showy plants mound 3-6' (0.9-1.8cm) high. Prefers rich, moist soil; healthy, established plants best left undisturbed. Attractive dark green leaves are deeply divided. Blue or blue-and-white flowers in spikes or clusters appear in late summer.

Note: all plant parts are poisonous; when cutting, avoid infecting open wounds.

Zones: 3-7, heat 8-3
Spacing: 18-24" (45-60cm)
Propagation: division of tuberous roots;
 seed (slow to germinate)

A. Xcammarum (ka-MAH-rum)
Bicolor Monkshood
Clusters of blue-edged white flowers in late summer and fall. Height 3-4' (0.9-1.2m).

A. carmichaelii (kar-mi-KAY-lee-y)
Azure Monkshood
Foliage thick and leathery. Spikes of deep blue flowers in late summer, early fall. Height 3-5' (0.9-1.5m).

A. napellus (na-PEL-lus)
Common Monkshood, Aconite Monkshood
Late summer flowers are dark blue. Narrow plants, 3-4' (0.9-1.2m) high. Space 12" (30cm). Zones 3-6.

Aconitum Xcammarum

Aconitum napellus

Aconitum carmichaelii

Adenophora confusa

Adiantum pedatum

Adonis amurensis

ADENOPHORA (a-den-OF-o-ra) ☼ ☁

Ladybells
Dainty plant looks somewhat like Canterbury Bells, though with more slender and branching stems. Needs well-drained soil; best left undisturbed. Leaves hug stems. Summer flowers are shades of blue, nodding and bell-shaped, borne in spikes.
Zones: 2-8
Spacing: 18-24" (45-60cm)
Propagation: seed

A. confusa (kon-FEW-sa)
Common Ladybells
Deep blue flowers, each about 3/4" (2cm) long. Height 24-30" (60-75cm).

A. liliifolia (li-lee-i-FOH-li-a)
Lilyleaf Ladybells
Pale blue flowers are 1/2" (1.3cm) long. Height to 24" (60cm).

ADIANTUM (a-dee-AN-tum) ☁ ☁ 🌲

A. pedatum (pe-DAH-tum)
Five-fingered Maidenhair,
American or Northern Maidenhair Fern
Dainty fern with pea-green leaflets on polished purple-brown stems. Easy to grow in moist yet well-drained humusy soil. Spreads slowly; deciduous or semi-evergreen. Naturalized. Several cultivars, growing 12-24" (30-60cm).
Zones: 3-8, heat 9-3
Spacing: 12-18" (30-45cm)
Propagation: division, spores

ADONIS (a-DOH-nis) ☼ ☁

Low-growing perennials effective in rock garden or massed at front of border. Light green, feathery foliage. Large, clear yellow, cup-shaped flowers on erect stems, from early spring to early summer. The annual adonis add reds and coppery tones. Prefers well-drained sandy loam soil.
Zones: 3-7
Spacing: 6-10" (15-25cm)
Propagation: seed, division

A. amurensis (a-moo-REN-sis)
Amur Adonis
Height 9-12" (23-30cm). Starts flowering early, as soon as frost is out of ground; yellow flowers are 2-3" (5-8cm) across, often more than one per stem. Foliage dies back in early summer. Tolerates dry soil.

A. vernalis (ver-NAH-lis)
Spring Adonis
Height 12-15" (30-38cm). Buttercup-yellow flowers from early spring, one per stem. Foliage persists until early fall.

Plant zones included in the descriptions are guides to a plant's ability to grow well in a given location with normal, average expected extremes of cold and heat.

AEGOPODIUM (ee-goh-POH-di-um)
Bishop's Weed
A. podagraria 'Variegatum'
   (poh-da-GRAH-ri-a ve-ri-e-GAH-tum)
Silveredge Bishop's Weed, Goutweed,
Snow-on-the-mountain
Versatile and hardy, fast-spreading ground cover grows
6-12" (15-30cm) high. Useful where little else will grow,
sun or shade, rich or poor soil. Leaves green with
silver margins. Insignificant white flowers in midsummer; remove to prevent self-seeding. May become invasive. Naturalized. Tolerates extra-moist soils.
Zones: 2-8
Spacing: 10-15" (25-38cm)
Propagation: division in spring or fall

AETHIONEMA (ee-thi-oh-NEE-ma)
Stonecress
A. armenum 'Warley Rose' (ar-MEE-num)
[A. Xwarleyense]
Warley Rose Stonecress
Low-growing shrubby evergreen grows 6-8" (15-20cm)
high. Prefers light, sandy soil. Good in rock gardens and
as edging or small area ground cover. Blue-green foliage. Flowers bright pink in spring. Shear back lightly
after flowering to encourage fresh new growth.
Zones: 5-7, heat 9-7
Spacing: 12-15" (30-38cm)
Propagation: seed, cuttings, division

Aegopodium podagraria 'Variegatum'

AGASTACHE
(a-gah-STAK-ee, a-gah-STASH-ee)
Agastache 'Blue Fortune'
Blue Fortune Hyssop
Compact, aromatic, gray-green perennial for border,
herb garden, background. Spikes of close-spaced blue
flowers with purplish-violet bracts in mid to late summer.
Fast growth to height of 2-4' (0.6-1.2m). Blossoms attract
bees, butterflies, hummingbirds. Native species. Tolerates very dry conditions.
Zones: 5-9, heat 12-5
Spacing: 15-24" (38-60cm)
Propagation: division in spring or fall

AJANIA (a-JAH-nee-a)
A. pacifica (pa-SIF-i-ka)
[Chrysanthemum pacificum (pa-SIF-i-kum)]
Silver-and-gold Chrysanthemum
Spreading perennial mounds to 12" (30cm) high, grows
to 36" (90cm) wide. Useful rock garden, container plant.
Silver-edged leaves. Clusters of small yellow flowers in
fall. Zones 5-9. Protect in zone 4 winters.
Zones: 4-10, heat 12-1
Spacing: 18-30" (45-75cm)
Propagation: division, seed

Agastache 'Blue Fortune'

Ajania pacifica

Aethionema armenum 'Warley Rose'

AJUGA (a-JOO-ga) ☼ ⛅ 〰

Bugleweed

Low, fast-growing ground cover. Thrives in almost any well-drained soil. Leaves form dense mat or mound. Full sun enhances foliage colors. Flowers from late spring to early summer.

Zones: 3-10, heat 8-2
Spacing: 12-18" (15-30cm)
Propagation: division, seed

A. genevensis (je-ne-VEN-sis)
Geneva Bugleweed
Mounding clumps rise 6-12" (15-30cm). Dark green, toothed leaves. Flower spikes to 2" (5cm) long, usually bright blue though may be pink or white. Good for rock gardens. Space 9" (23cm).

A. pyramidalis (pi-ra-mi-DAH-lis)
Upright Bugleweed
Forms clumps 6-9" (15-23cm) high and wide. Dark foliage is smoother than that of *A. genevensis*. Blue flowers in 4-6" (10-15cm) spikes. Space 9" (23cm).

A. reptans (REP-tanz)
Carpet Bugle
Very low growing, spreads rapidly by means of stolons (stems); height 4-12" (10-30cm). Leaf color, form variable; flowers blue or purple.

'Burgundy Glow': foliage shades of white, pink, rose, and green; turn deep bronze in fall; younger leaves have rosy hue.

'Catlin's Giant': one of the largest; bronze-green leaves grow to 8" (20cm); blue flowers

'Cristata': one of several forms with crinkled leaves.

'Gaiety': bronze-purple leaves; lilac flowers.

'Jungle Beauty': leaves variegated cream and purplish-green, tinted red and pink. Remove plain dark purple-green parts to maintain multi-colored growth.

'Pink Beauty': deep pink flowers on long spikes; leaves green.

'Silver Beauty': gray-green leaves are edged white.

a

Ajuga reptans 'Pink Beauty'

Ajuga genevensis

Ajuga reptans

Ajuga reptans 'Catlins Giant'

Ajuga reptans 'Gaiety'

Ajuga reptans 'Pink Beauty'

Ajuga reptans 'Silver Beauty'

ALCEA (al-SEE-a) ☀ ✄ 🦋 🐦

A. rosea (ROH-zee-a)
Garden Hollyhock
Biennials or shortlived perennials, usually reseed spontaneously. Plant at back or center of border, or grow against fence or wall. Bright green leaves are felt-like and hairy. Flower spikes rise 4-9' (1.2-2.7m). Individual blossoms 3-5" (8-13cm) across; single, ruffled, frilled, or double blooms in nearly every shade of white, pink, yellow and lavender. Best in moist though well-drained soil, with good air circulation.

> **'Chater's Double':** ruffled, ball-shaped, double flowers in scarlet, pink, white and yellow. Height 4-6' (1.2-1.8m).

> **'Powderpuffs':** large double flowers on spikes 4-5' (1.2-1.5m) tall; colors are yellow, white, pink, scarlet and salmon.

Zones: 3-8, heat 10-3
Spacing: 15-18" (38-45cm)
Propagation: seed

Alcea rosea

ALCHEMILLA (al-ke-MIL-a) ☁ ☁ ✄

Lady's-mantle
Low-growing perennial for shady areas. Large rounded or lobed leaves are grayish light green. Flowers in spring; greenish yellow clusters of petalless blossoms readily scatter seeds to expand spread. Best with consistent soil moisture.
Zones: 3-10, heat 7-1
Spacing: 10-12" (25-30cm)
Propagation: seed, division

A. alpina (al-PY-na) 〰
Mountain Lady's-mantle
Dwarf habit, good for ground cover in no-traffic areas. Height 6-8" (15-20cm). Deeply cut 2" (5cm) green leaves have silvery margins.

A. erythropoda (ee-ri-throh-POH-da) 〰
Dwarf Lady's-mantle
Mounds to about 8" (20cm). Small, scalloped, blue-green leaves, lime-green flowers in spring. Prefers cool, moist summers.

A. mollis (MOL-is)
Common Lady's-mantle
Height 12-18" (30-45cm). Leaves have shallow lobes. Flowers in early summer, chartreuse-colored starry clusters. Space 18-24" (45-60cm).

Alcea rosea

Alchemilla mollis

Amsonia tabernaemontana

Allium schoenoprasum

Anacyclus pyrethrum var. *depressus*

ALLIUM (AL-i-um) ☼ ☁ 🦋
Ornamental Onion

Decorative relatives of the onion, useful in border or rock garden and as edging plants. Best in full sun. Plant to depth of three times bulb diameter, in well-drained soil. Foliage dies back during or after blooming. Typical onion smell only when plant tissues are cut or crushed.
Zones: 4-9, heat 9-5
Spacing: varies with size of species
Propagation: seed, division

A. sativum (sa-TEE-vum)
Garlic

Height to 24" (60cm), leaves to 1" (2.5cm) wide, flowers pinkish. Bulblets (cloves) used for flavoring. Usually grown as annual with bulbs lifted in summer or fall.

A. schoenoprasum (shoh-noh-PRAY-sum)
Chives

Useful edging or mid-border species, to 24" (60cm) tall. Gray-green leaves are tasty when cut into salads and for cooking. Rose-purple flower clusters in summer. Space 4-6" (10-15cm). Spreads rapidly in rich, moist soil. Plant at soil level.

AMSONIA (am-SOH-ni-a) ☁
Bluestar

A. tabernaemontana (ta-ber-nee-mon-TAH-na)
Willow Amsonia, Blue Star Flower

Low maintenance perennial for borders and natural plantings. Height 12-36" (30-90cm). Grows well in moist, cool places; tolerates dry soil, full sun, though with reduced vigor. Willow-like leaves are gray-green. Flowers steel blue, borne in terminal clusters in late spring. Naturalized.
Zones: 3-9, heat 8-4
Spacing: 18-24" (45-60cm)
Propagation: seed, division in spring or fall

ANACYCLUS (a-na-SYK-lus) ☼ ⋙
A. pyrethrum var. *depressus*
(py-REE-thrum, de-PRES-us)
[A. depressus]
Mount Atlas Daisy

Low-growing perennial grows 4-8" (10-20cm) high. Daisy blossoms open from crimson buds, have yellow centers and white petals with red undersides. Flowers close up in dull weather. Dislikes humidity: rots in heavy, moist soils.
Zones: 5-7
Spacing: 6-12" (45-60cm)
Propagation: seed, softwood cuttings in spring

ANAPHALIS (a-NAH-fa-lis) ☼ ✂
A. triplinervis (tri-pli-NER-vis)
Pearly Everlasting
Compact, easy gray-green plant mounds 12-24" (30-60cm). Best in evenly moist soil. Good for naturalizing; tolerates drought, partial shade. Leaves have dense white furry covering. Masses of small white flowers from summer until frost. Excellent for cutting and drying.
Zones: 3-8, heat 8-3
Spacing: 9-12" (23-30cm)
Propagation: division, seed

ANCHUSA (an-KOO-sa) ☼
Alkanet, Bugloss
A. azurea (a-ZEW-ree-a)
Italian Bugloss
Short lived, selfseeding perennials with crisp blue flowers. Height 3-5' (0.9-1.5m); grows well in any soil except in wet conditions. Will tolerate some shade. Loosely structured plants may require support. Leaves hairy, 4-8" (10-20cm) long. Flowers bright blue, in one-sided clusters. Colorful filler plants among more formal perennials.
  'Little John': dark blue flowers; compact growth to 18" (45cm).
  'Loddon Royalist': gentian-blue flowers on 36" (90cm) plants.
Zones: 3-8, heat 8-1
Spacing: 18-24" (45-60cm)
Propagation: division, root cuttings, seed

ANEMONE (a-NEM-oh-nee) ⛅ ✂
Showy plants with a variety of different forms and colors. Compound or divided leaves, and petalless flowers. Color is provided by showy sepals. Grow in any well-drained soil. Shelter from afternoon sun.
Zones: 4-8, heat 9-3
Spacing: varies by species
Propagation: division, root cuttings, seed

A. canadensis (ka-na-DEN-sis)
Meadow Anemone
White flowers top plants in summer. Light green, segmented foliage contrasts well with darker shrubs, ever-

Anchusa azurea

Anaphalis triplinervis

Anaphalis triplinervis

Anemone sylvestris

Anemone tomentosa

Anemone X*hybrida*

Antennaria dioica

greens. Naturalized. Height 12-24" (30-60cm). Spreads; space 12-18" (30-45cm). Hardy to zone 3.

A. Xhybrida (HYB-ri-da)
Japanese Anemone, Windflower
Late summer flowers may be pink or white, single or double. Foliage light green. Height 30-36" (75-90cm). Space 18" (45cm).
   'Honorine Jobert': white flowers, 3-4' (0.9-1.2m) tall, prolific.

A. sylvestris (sil-VES-tris)
Snowdrop Anemone
White spring flowers followed by fluffy white fruits. Foliage light green. Height 10-18" (25-45cm). Best in partial shade. Space 12" (30cm).

A. tomentosa (toh-men-TOH-sa)
[*A. vitifolia* (vi-ti-FOH-li-a)]
Grape-leaf Anemone
Fall blooming anemone has dark green lobed leaves and white flowers. Stoloniferous plants form clumps 18-36" (45-90cm) high. Space 18" (45cm).

ANTENNARIA (an-te-NAH-ri-a) ☼ ⌇
Pussy-toes
A. dioica (dy-OH-i-ka)
Pussy-toes, Rose Pussy-toes
Rapidly spreading mat of 1" (2.5cm) gray-green or silver leaves. Tolerates poor soil and dry conditions. Useful as a quick filler; contain spread by dividing plants. Pinkish tips on light green flower clusters resemble cat's toes. Flowers in late spring.
   'Rosea' [*A. dioica* var. *rosea* (ROH-zee-a), *A. rosea*]: rose-red flowers on stems 8-10" (20-25cm) high.
   'Tomentosa' [*A. tomentosa* (toh-men-TOH-sa)]: creamy white flower clusters rise only to 3" (8cm).
Zones: 3-8, heat 7-1
Spacing: 10-15" (25-38cm)
Propagation: division in spring, seed

A warm, protected planting site often extends the northern limit of a plant's hardiness zones. Sheltered, cool, and somewhat moist locations may extend to the south a zone's southern limit.

ANTHEMIS (AN-the-mis) ☀ 🌲 ✂
Golden Marguerite
Showy mounds with bright yellow or orange (sometimes white) daisies and aromatic, finely divided foliage. Tolerates poor soil; excessive fertilizer may result in unsightly growth. Useful for cutting during summer; trim off old flowers to encourage fresh blossoms.
Zones: hardiness varies by species; heat 8-3
Spacing: 12-24" (30-60cm)
Propagation: division every 2-3 years, seed

A. marschalliana (mar-shal-ee-AH-na)
[*A. biebersteiniana* (bee-ber-sty-nee-AH-na)]
Marshall Chamomile
Golden-yellow flowers top silvery foliage. Smaller than many Anthemis species: height 12-18" (30-45cm). Useful in rock gardens. Zones 5-7.

A. tinctoria (tink-TOH-ri-a)
Golden Marguerite
Excellent border plant, 24-36" (60-90cm) high. May need staking in rich soils. Flowers yellow, about 1½" (4cm) across. Cut back hard after flowering to encourage new growth. Zones 3-7.
  'E. C. Buxton': flowers off-white with lemon yellow centers; height to 30" (75cm).
  'Kelwayi': bright golden yellow flowers.

Anthemis tinctoria

AQUILEGIA (ak-wi-LEE-ji-a)
Columbine ☀ ☁ ✂ 🦋 🦅
Distinctive mounds of airy, fan-like leaves contrast with pastel flowers. Best with good moisture supply in well-drained, rich soil. Needs partial shade in hot dry areas. Dainty, multi-colored, spurred blossoms attract humming-birds in spring and early summer. Mulch plants in zones 3-5 from late fall to early spring to prevent heaving.
Zones: 3-9, heat 9-3
Spacing: 10-15" (25-38cm)
Propagation: seed

Aquilegia X*hybrida*

Aquilegia caerulea

Aquilegia canadensis

Aquilegia flabellata

Aquilegia chrysantha

Aquilegia X*hybrida* 'Nora Barlow'

A. caerulea (se-REW-lee-a)
American, Blue, or Colorado Columbine
Blue-purple or white flowers in early summer. Naturalized. Height 12-24" (30-60cm), spread 24" (60cm). Space 18-24" (45-60cm). Zones 3-8.

A. canadensis (ka-na-DEN-sis)
Wild Columbine
Early spring red-and-yellow blossoms on 12-36" (30-90cm) plants. Best in moist, shady locations. Naturalized. Zones 3-8.

A. chrysantha (kri-SAN-tha)
Golden Columbine
Yellow flowers in spring. Height 30-42" (75-100cm). Plants may need staking for support. Naturalized. Zones 4-8.

A. flabellata (fla-be-LAH-ta)
Fan Columbine
Shorter plant with blue-purple, lilac, white or bicolor flowers. Height 8-18" (20-45cm). Use for border front and rock garden. Leaf segments often overlap and are darker green than those of other columbines.

A. formosa (for-MOH-sa)
Sitka, Red, Western, or California Columbine
Red and yellow flowers from early summer. Grows to 36" (90cm).

A. Xhybrida (HYB-ri-da)
Hybrid Columbine
Blooms late spring to early summer; big, large showy flowers, wide color range.

   'Biedermeier', Nosegay Columbine: compact plants 9-12" (23-30cm) tall; flowers mostly blue and white.
   'Dragon Fly': mixed colors; height 18-24" (45-60cm)
   'McKana Hybrids': showy hybrids have abundant, colorful large flowers with long, flared spurs; height 30-36" (75-90cm).
   'Music': many colors available; height 18-20" (45-50cm).
   'Nora Barlow': fully double flowers look like small dahlias; color reddish pink, edged white; height 24-30" (60-75cm).

ARABIS (AR-a-bis) ☼ ⌇ ♠ ☙
Rock Cress
Low, spreading evergreen perennial prefers cooler climates. Best in well-drained soil. Good edging, rock garden plant. Flowers white, pink.
Zones: 3-7, heat 8-1
Spacing: 9-15" (23-38cm)
Propagation: division, cuttings, seed

A. blepharophylla (ble-fa-roh-FIL-a)
Fringed Rock Cress
Flat rosettes of dark green leaves. Fragrant rose-purple spring flowers. Height 4-8" (10-20cm). Tender plant; give winter protection in north. Naturalized.
   'Spring Charm': rose-tinted flowers. Zones 5-7.

A. caucasica (kaw-KAS-i-ka)
[*A. albida* (AL-bi-da)]
Wall Rock Cress
Spreading plant forms loose mat with succulent, whitish-green leaves. Prolific white flowers in spring. Excellent on walls, in rock gardens. Height 8-15" (20-38cm). Cut back hard after flowering to encourage thicker new growth. To renew, divide vigorous clumps every 2-3 years.
   'Snow Cap': large white ornamental blossoms.
   'Flore Pleno': double white flowers; height to 12" (30cm).
   'Variegata': green leaves with yellow-white striping and edging.

A. ferdinandi-coburgii 'Variegata'
   (fer-di-NAN-dee koh-BER-gee)
Variegated Rock Cress, Ferdinand's Rock Cress
Tightly clumping mat of succulent, ivory-edged leaves. Flowers white, prolific. Mounds 4-6" (10-15cm) with 8-10" (20-25cm) spread.

Arabis blepharophylla 'Spring Charm'

Arabis caucasica

Arabis caucasica 'Variegata'

Arenaria montana

Arisaema triphyllum

Armeria maritima

ARENARIA (a-re-NAH-ri-a)
Sandwort
Forms low, trailing mat of dense foliage. Prolific white flowers in early summer. Excellent for rock gardens.
Zones: 4-8, heat 9-6
Spacing: 10-12" (25-30cm)
Propagation: seed, division, cuttings

A. montana (mon-TAH-na)
Mountain Sandwort
Glossy green leaves and big 1" (2.5cm) white flowers. Best in slightly acid soil. Tolerates moist soils. Height 2-4" (5-10cm).

A. verna (VER-na)
[*A. caespitosa* (sez-pi-TOH-sa)]
Moss Sandwort
Fine, moss-like evergreen leaves. Grows rapidly in sun or part shade. Late spring flowers are white, star-like, 1/2" (1.3cm) across.

ARISAEMA (a-ris-EE-ma)
A. triphyllum (try-FIL-um)
Jack-in-the-pulpit
Tuberous perennial with large green to purple spathe or sheath surrounding flower spike (spadix). Prefers fertile, moist yet well-drained soil. Height 16-20" (40-50cm). Leaves three-lobed. Flowers in spring; bright red berries in fall.
Note: all plant parts are poisonous.
Zones: 4-9
Spacing: 12-18" (30-45cm)
Propagation: seed, division

ARMERIA (ah-MEE-ri-a)
Thrift, Sea Pink
A. maritima (ma-RIT-i-ma)
Common Thrift
Tufts of blue-green narrow leaves form spreading clumps that mound 6-12" (15-30cm). Tolerates seaside garden conditions. Best in light, sandy, well-drained soil. Good for rock garden, edging, or front of border. Flowers in summer; masses of ball-shaped clusters of pink, mauve-red, lilac, or white blossoms rise above foliage. Plants benefit from afternoon shade in southern gardens.
Zones: 4-8, heat 9-4
Spacing: 9-12" (23-30cm)
Propagation: division, seed

☀ = Full Sun   ✂ = Cut Flowers
⛅ = Partial Sun/Shade   🌲 = Evergreen
☁ = Shade   🦋 = attracts Butterflies
〜 = Groundcover   = attracts Hummingbirds

ARRHENATHERUM (a-re-NATH-e-rum)
A. elatius var. *bulbosum*
(e-LAH-ti-us bul-BOH-sum)
Tuber Oat Grass
Oat-like grass with broad, cascading leaf-blades about 12" (30cm) long. Clumps mound to 2-4' (0.6-1.2m). Purplish-green, narrow flower clusters on tall stems. Tuberous roots. Thrives in any fertile soil; tolerates drought when established. Grows best with cooler spring and fall temperatures. Naturalized.
'Variegatum': ivory leaf margins.
Zones: 4-9, heat 12-8
Spacing: 15" (38cm)
Propagation: division

Single color plantings are eye-catching and effective. For a cool, relaxing blue, try delphiniums and monkshood, bordered with blue-green hostas. Candidates for blue borders include flax, Canterbury bells, silver-leaved *Artemisia*, forget-me-not, globe thistle, gentian, iris, lavender, lilyturf, Virginia bluebells, and the sages.

Arrhenatherum elatius var. *bulbosum* 'Variegatum'

Artemisia 'Powis Castle'

ARTEMISIA (ar-te-MIZ-i-a)
Wormwood
Useful edging and border plants with silvery, fern-like, aromatic foliage that may persist through winter. Thrive in poor soils; tolerate drought. Good in hot climates and where winter conditions remain dry. Excess moisture can cause rotting, and over-fertilization results in unsightly growth. Flowers usually inconspicuous.
Zones: hardiness 3-9, may vary by species; heat 12-8
Spacing: 15-24" (38-90cm)
Propagation: division, cuttings, seed

A. 'Powis Castle': fine textured vigorous evergreen grows to 36" (90cm).

A. absinthium (ab-SIN-thi-um)
Common Wormwood, Absinthe
Silvery gray, finely divided foliage mounds 24-36" (60-90cm) by 24" (60cm) wide. Tiny gray flowers appear in late summer. Naturalized. Dried leaves sometimes used medicinally.
'Lambrook Silver': good accent 30" (75cm) high; cut back in summer to encourage dense new growth.

Artemisia lactiflora 'Guizho'

Artemisia dracunculus

Artemisia ludoviciana 'Valerie Finnis'

Artemisia ludoviciana 'Silver Queen'

Artemisia schmidtiana

A. dracunculus (dra-KUN-kew-lus) ✄
Tarragon
Upright, gray-green herb used as background for lower-growing plants and source of culinary tarragon. Height 18" (45cm). Zones 5-8.
A. dracunculus var. sativa (sa-TY-va), French Tarragon: flavorful leaves used in cooking and in perfumery.

A. lactiflora (lak-ti-FLOH-ra) ✄
White Mugwort
Creamy-white flowers appear mid-late summer to fall, in big, long-lasting, plume-like clusters. Foliage provide good foil for flowers. Height 4-6' (1.2-1.8m). Space 24-36" (60-90cm). Tolerates part shade. Zones 3-8.
   'Guizho': very dark green foliage on almost black stems, distinctive contrast with creamy flowers. Best in rich, fertile soil.

Many border plants are grown for foliage rather than flower beauty. For example, *Artemisia* species and varieties make more compact and bushy growth if flower buds are trimmed off.

A. ludoviciana (loo-doh-vik-ee-AH-na) ✄
White Sage
Compact plant with 2-4" (5-10cm) silvery-gray leaves on whitish stems. Late summer flowers. Naturalized. Height 2-4' (0.6-1.2m).
   'Silver King': deep silver leaves; flower plumes show unusual red color in fall.
   'Silver Queen': silvery foliage has deeply cut margins.
   'Valerie Finnis': big silvery-gray leaves; height 15-18" (38-45cm).

A. schmidtiana (shmit-ee-AH-na) ⋎⋏
Satiny Wormwood, Silver Mound Artemisia
Mounding intense silver-gray plant with satiny, finely cut leaves. Height 15-24" (38-60cm). Summer flowers small and yellow. Best when trimmed before flowers fully develop, to maintain mound form. Usually available in compact forms known as **'Nana'** or **'Silver Mound'** with height of 6-12" (15-30cm). Space 10-15" (25-38cm).

ARUNCUS (a-RUN-kus) ☀ ⛅
Goatsbeard
Stately, shrub-like perennials that produce creamy-white plumes of blossom in early summer. Forms large yet non-invasive clumps in rich soil. Best with shade and moisture in southern areas, full sun in north. Leaves compound (unlike those of Astilbe, which, with divided leaves, look similar). Male and female flowers on different plants.
Zones: 3-7, heat 10-1
Spacing: 3-5' (0.9-1.5m); smaller selections 18-24" (45-60cm)
Propagation: division, seed

A. aethusifolius (ee-thoo-si-FOH-li-us)
Miniature Goatsbeard
True miniature, growing just 8-12" (20-30cm). Good for rock garden, front of border. Tolerates partial shade. Leaves deeply cut.

A. dioicus (dy-OH-i-kus)
[*A. sylvester* (sil-VES-ter)]
Goatsbeard
Flower plumes rise 4-6' (1.2-1.8m) in late spring. Leaves extend 24-36" (60-90cm) long. Naturalized.
   'Kneiffii': grows only 24-36" (60-90cm) tall, has finely dissected compound leaves; space more closely.

ASARUM (a-SAH-rum) ☁ 〰
Wild Ginger
Rhizomatous perennials with fleshy, sometimes ever-green leaves that shelter pitcher-shaped flowers. Need rich, moist yet well-drained soil. Useful ground cover in damp, shaded area.
Zones: hardiness varies by species; heat zones 9-3
Spacing: 6-10" (15-25cm)
Propagation: division, seed

A. canadense (ka-na-DEN-see)
Wild Ginger, Snakeroot
Heart-shaped leaves are about 6" (15cm) wide. Height 4-6" (10-15cm). Naturalized. Hardy in zones 3-7.

Aruncus aethusifolius

Asarum canadense

Aruncus dioicus

Asarum europaeum

Asclepias incarnata 'Alba'

Asclepias tuberosa

Asclepias incarnata

Asclepias tuberosa

A. europaeum (ew-roh-PAY-um) 🌲
European Wild Ginger
Dark green, glossy evergreen leaves 2-3" (5-8cm) wide.
Height 4-6" (10-15cm). Zones 4-7.

A. shuttleworthii (shut-el-WUR-thee-y)
Mottled or Southern Wild Ginger
Leaves broad, often mottled with silvery markings.
Height to 8" (20cm). Naturalized. Zones 5-8.

A. virginicum (vir-JIN-i-kum) 🌲
Virginia Wild Ginger
Evergreen wild ginger grows to 7" (17.5cm). Dark green
leaves with some white spotting. Zones 3-7.

When perennial growth slows and foliage starts to
yellow and dry, reduce watering frequency even in dry
climates. But don't stop watering altogether until plants
are dormant or after all top growth has died back — the
roots and stems below ground continue to develop and,
in many cases, to store food for next season's growth.

ASCLEPIAS (as-KLEE-pi-as) ☼ ✄ 🦋 🐦
Milkweed
Upright and vigorous, tuberous-rooted perennials with
narrow foliage and milky sap. Best in well-drained sandy,
fertile soil. Both flowers and dried seedpods useful for
cut arrangements. Naturalized.
Zones: 4-9, heat 10-2
Spacing: 18-24" (45-60cm)
Propagation: seed, division

A. incarnata (in-kar-NAH-ta) 🦋
Swamp Milkweed
Clusters of pink to white flowers. Attracts butterflies.
Easy to grow; tolerates wet soils. Height 3-4' (0.9-1.2m).
Best in zones 3-7.

A. tuberosa (tew-be-ROH-sa) 🦋
Butterfly Flower
Showy bright orange flowers in summer attract Mon-
arch butterflies. Grows 24-42" (60-105cm) tall. Tolerates
dry, infertile soils.

ASTER (AS-ter) ☼ ✄ 🦋

Mounding or open habit perennials with colorful, yellow-centered daisy flowers. Best in well-drained soil. Heights range from 6" (15cm) to 6' (1.8m). Taller asters usually require staking for support. Encourage branching by pinching new growth in spring and early summer.
Zones: 3-8, heat 9-1
Spacing: 12-24" (30-60cm), more for larger varieties
Propagation: division, cuttings, seed (species)

A. alpinus (al-PY-nus)
Alpine Aster
Summer-flowering rock garden, front or edging plant for cooler areas. Flowers purple. Height 6-9" (15-23cm). Gray-green foliage turns green in summer. Zones 4-7.
   'Goliath': light blue flowers; height to 15" (38cm).

When planting near a wall or building, remember to leave space for air circulation behind the plants. A three-foot (ninety centimeter) or greater gap allows access behind young plants for weeding and cultivation. It also protects them from excessive buildup of reflected heat.

A. dumosus (doo-MOH-sus)
[*A. novae-angliae* (NOH-vay-AN-glee-ay)]
Hardy Compact Aster
Vigorously branching perennials form neat, attractive mounds. Colorful daisy flowers from late summer. Use in mixed border, for edging. Naturalized. Many cultivars with various flower colors.
   'Wood's Light Blue': clear pale blue flowers. Height 12-16" (30-40cm). Dark green, rust resistant foliage.
   'Wood's Pink': clear pink flowers. Mounds 12-16" (30-40cm).
   'Wood's Purple': Purple flowers. Mounds 12-16" (30-40cm) high.

A. Xfrikartii (fri-KAR-tee-y)
Frikart's Aster
Lavender blossoms in summer on 24-36" (60-90cm) plants. Informal, open habit. Space 24-36" (60-90cm). Mildew resistant dark green leaves.
   'Mönch': sturdy plants spread 36" (90cm).

Aster alpinus

Aster dumosus 'Wood's Pink'

Aster dumosus 'Wood's Light Blue'

Aster Xfrikartii

Aster Xfrikartii 'Mönch'

Aster novi-belgii

Aster novae-angliae 'Alma Potschke'

A. lateriflorus (la-ti-FLOH-rus) 〰
[*A. lateriflorus* var. *horizontalis* (ho-ri-zon-TAH-lis)]
Calico Aster
Small daisy flowers on many-branched spreading mound. Dark green leaves turn purplish for fall flowering time. Height and spread 24-36" (60-90cm). Naturalized. Varieties in white, cream or pale blue; red-brown centers.

A. novae-angliae (NOH-vay-AN-glee-ay)
New England Aster
Many cultivars available, with wide color range. Vigorously branching plants grow 3-6' (0.9-1.8m) tall. Flower in late summer; species has violet-purple blossoms, 1½-2" (4-5cm) across. Good for cutting. Naturalized.
    'Alma Potschke': vivid salmon pink flowers; height to 4' (1.2m).
    'Purple Dome': abundant blue-purple flowers on compact, 18-24" (45-60cm) plants.

A. novi-belgii (NOH-vee-BEL-jee-y)
Michaelmas Daisy, New York Aster
Many cultivars with 1" (2.5cm) blossoms in shades of lilac, blue, pink, red. Species is violet. Flower in late summer; good for cutting. Small, or dwarf varieties grow to 15" (38cm) high; medium varieties grow to 4' (1.2m); tall varieties reach height of 6' (1.8m). Naturalized.

A. tongolensis (ton-go-LEN-sis)
East Indies Aster
Short, vigorously spreading species produces 2" (5cm) flowers in summer on strong stems that need no support. Grows 12-24" (30-60cm) high, spreads to 12" (30cm). Flowers are violet-blue with bright orange centers. Divide plants after flowering to maintain vigor.

Water herbaceous perennials during dry spells. Give sufficient water to penetrate the ground to some depth, for a mere sprinkling will encourage the growth of surface roots that succumb rapidly to continued drought. A summer mulch helps retain soil moisture.

ASTILBE (a-STIL-bee) ☼ ☁ ✄ 🦋

Summer-flowering perennials that thrive in shaded, moist locations. White, pink, red, or purple flower clusters rise in fluffy plumes over mounded green foliage. Leaves may have coppery color when young. Flowers good for cutting: harvest when half open for use fresh or to dry for winter decoration. Plant with 'eye' just below surface of deep, rich soil; water and fertilize well. Intolerant of drought while growing, and too much moisture in winter. Divide healthy plants every three or four years.

Zones: 4-9, heat 8-2
Spacing: 18-24" (45-60cm)
Propagation: division

A. Xarendsii (a-REND-zee-y)
Astilbe, False Spirea
Many cultivars flowering in mid to late summer, with colors that range from clear white to blood red. Foliage colors from copper to dark green. Height 2-4' (0.6-1.2m). Best in moist but not soggy soil.

'Bridal Veil' ['Brautschleier']: White flowers with faint pink tinge, strong green foliage; height to 28" (70cm).

'Etna': Dark red midsummer flowers; 18-24" (45-60cm) tall.

'Fanal': dark, blood red flowers and dark bronze leaves; grows to 24" (60cm).

A. chinensis (chi-NEN-sis)
Chinese Astilbe
Summer flowers are light pink to light purple on 18-36" (45-90cm) plants. Foliage deeply cut, bronze green. Somewhat drought tolerant.

'Finale': light pink flowers cluster on 15-18" (38-45cm) plants.

'Pumila': grows just 8-12" (20-30cm) high and is good for rock gardens and front of borders. Lavender pink flowers.

'Visions': Pale purple flowers; 12-14" (30-35cm) tall.

A. chinensis var. taguetii (tar-GET-ee-y)
[A. taguetii]
Fall Astilbe
Late summer flowering astilbe with excellent vase life when cut. Lilac colored blossoms followed by attractive fruits that remain all winter. Height 2-4' (0.6-1.2m).

'Superba': blooms into early fall; flowers magenta or red-purple, rise 3-5' (0.9-1.5m). Foliage bronze green.

A. japonica (ja-PON-i-ka)
Pyramidal clusters of small flowers above compound, sometimes variegated leaves. Height 24-36" (60-90cm). Supply ample water during growth.

'Deutschland': white; early summer, height to 24" (60cm).

'Rheinland': clear pink flowers; height to 24" (60cm).

'Peach Blossom': delicate pink flowers; height to 24" (60cm).

'Red Sentinel': scarlet red plumes rise over bronze-green foliage.

A. simplicifolia (sim-pli-si-FOH-li-a)
Star Astilbe
Star-like flowers on dwarf 12-18" (30-45cm) plants. Colors from white to carmine. Forms compact mounds. Glossy leaves not divided.

'Aphrodite': salmon-red flowers; height 15-20" (38-50cm).

'Hennie Graafland': upright trusses of delicate pink flowers; grows to 16" (40cm).

'Bronze Elegance': clear, darker pink flowers open late over bronze-tinted foliage; height 12-16" (30-40cm).

'Sprite' (1994 Perennial Plant of the Year): airy shell-pink flowers and attractive rust-colored fruits.

a

Astilbe ✕*arendsii* 'Bridal Veil'

Astilbe ✕*arendsii* 'Fanal'

Astilbe chinensis 'Finale'

Astilbe chinensis 'Pumila'

Astilbe chinensis 'Visions'

Astilbe chinensis
var. *taguetii* 'Superba'

Astilbe japonica 'Deutschland'

Astilbe japonica 'Rheinland'

Astilbe japonica 'Red Sentinel'

Astilbe simplicifolia 'Aphrodite'

Astilbe simplicifolia
'Bronze Elegance'

Astilbe simplicifolia 'Sprite'

ASTRANTIA (as-TRAN-shi-a)
Masterwort
A. major (MAY-jor)
Astrantia, Greater Masterwort
Late spring flowering perennials for shaded, moist locations. Clusters of greenish-white to rose-pink flowers; papery bracts often tinted purple. Cultivars offer various colors and variegated leaves. Height 24-36" (60-90cm), spreads 18" (45cm). Flowers good for cutting, for use fresh or to dry for winter decoration. Plant in humus-rich soil and supply ample water during the growing season. Best where nights are cool. Easy to grow, spread quickly. Divide crowded plants in spring or fall.
Zones: 4-7, heat 7-1
Spacing: 15-18" (38-45cm)
Propagation: division, seed

ATHYRIUM (a-THI-ri-um)
Deciduous ferns with arching fronds. Best in moist, humus-rich soil.
Zones: 4-9, heat 8-1
Spacing: 12-24" (30-60cm)
Propagation: division, spores

A. filix-femina (FIL-iks-FEM-i-na)
Lady Fern
Pale green fronds. Height 2-4' (0.6-1.2m). Tolerates some sun. Many named cultivars offer variety of forms and sizes. Naturalized.

A. nipponicum 'Pictum' (ni-PON-i-kum PIK-tum)
Japanese Painted Fern
Silvery gray-and-green fronds on red-purple stems. Grows 12-18" (30-45cm) high.

AUBRIETA (aw-bree-AY-ta)
A. deltoidea (del-TOI-dee-a)
Rock Cress
Compact, spreading perennials for rock gardens, edging, and front of borders. Mounds 6-8" (15-20cm). Best in well-drained soil, in full sun except in hot areas. Flowers from spring to early summer; blue, pink, red, violet or purple. Cut back after flowering, spreading thin layer of fertile topsoil or compost over plants to encourage dense new growth.
Zones: 4-9
Spacing: 15-18" (38-45cm)
Propagation: seed, division, cuttings

When spring sunlight is strong enough to warm the soil surface, remove winter mulches and prick or cultivate the top inch or two between herbaceous perennials and other plants. The first fertilizer may now be applied. At the same time, check for snails, slugs, and other pests; remove plant debris so new growth won't be infected or infested with any disease or pest that have survived winter's cold.

Astrantia major

Athyrium filix-femina

Athyrium nipponicum 'Pictum'

Aubretia deltoidea

Aurinia saxatilis 'Compacta'

Baptisia australis

AURINIA (aw-RIN-i-a) ☀ ⛅ ⌇

A. saxatilis (sak-SAT-i-lis)
[*Alyssum saxatile* (a-LIS-sum sak-SAT-i-lee)]
Basket-of-gold
Fast-growing rock garden, wall, or front of border plant
thrives in full sun. Mounds 6-12" (15-30cm). Gray-green
foliage. Brilliant yellow flowers in tight clusters, from early
spring to early summer. Trim to shape after flowering.
  'Citrina' ['Sulphurea']: lemon-yellow flowers on
  12-15" (30-38cm) mounds.
  'Compacta': bright golden-yellow flowers; compact
  plants that mound 8-10" (20-25cm) high.
Zones: 3-7, heat 9-2
Spacing: 12" (30cm)
Propagation: softwood cuttings, division, seed

> Plant perennials with weed-free rootstocks, and keep
> them as weed-free as possible. Once weeds become
> established among close-knit perennial roots, it is
> almost impossible to remove them without destroying
> the specimens.

BAPTISIA (bap-TIZ-i-a) ☀ ⛅ 🦋 ✂

False Indigo, Wild Indigo
Bushy plants grow 3-5' (0.9-1.5m) tall. Best in deep rich,
neutral to acid soil, with good moisture supply: will tol-
erate poorer soils. Among the earliest of perennials to
emerge each spring. Leaflets in threes, rich bluish-green.
Loose clusters of pea-like flowers.
Zones: 3-9, heat 9-2
Spacing: see individual species
Propagation: seed, division

B. australis (aw-STRAH-lis)
Blue False Indigo
Blue flowers from late spring. Bushy plants form sea-
sonal hedge or screen. Naturalized. Space 36" (90cm).

B. tinctoria (tink-TOH-ri-a)
Yellow False Indigo, Horsefly Weed
Yellow flowers in summer. Tolerates neglect and periods
of drought. Good for natural plantings. Slender plants.
Space 10-12" (25-30cm).

BELAMCANDA (bel-am-KAN-da)
B. chinensis (chi-NEN-sis)
Blackberry Lily, Leopard Lily

Showy orange flowers with darker markings. Six-petaled blossoms open in succession on branched stems, mid to late summer. Black seed clusters good for fall arrangements. Iris-like foliage. Height to 36" (90cm). Mulch for winter in cooler zones (5-7).

Zones: 5-10
Spacing: 18-24" (45-60cm)
Propagation: seed, division

BELLIS (BEL-is)
B. perennis (pe-REN-nis)
English Daisy

Tender perennial, treated as a biennial or annual in northern zones. Needs well-drained soil. Good for edging and in rock gardens. Dark green leaves in 6" (15cm) clumps. Flowers in early spring; white, pink, or red daisies are 1-2" (2.5-5cm) across. Remove dead flowers regularly to encourage more bloom. In zones 3-5, lift plants and hold through winter under straw in cold frame. Elsewhere, lift and divide plants every two years to maintain vigor.

Zones: 6-10, heat 8-1
Spacing: 9-15" (20-25cm)
Propagation: seed, division

BERGENIA (ber-GEN-i-a)
B. cordifolia (kor-di-FOH-li-a)
Heartleaf Bergenia

Vigorous, spreading, large-leaved perennial makes good ground cover, border, or rock garden plant. Foliage grows 10" (25cm) across, glossy green turning deep burgundy in cold weather. Grows in any good garden soil; tolerates moisture. Early spring flowers rise in showy clusters. Plants mound 12-18" (30-45cm).

'Bressingham White': pink-colored blooms become pure white as they open and mature.
'Morning Red': dark purplish-red flowers; bronze-green foliage; lower growing mound, 8-12" (20-30cm) high.

Belamcanda chinensis

Bellis perennis

Bergenia cordifolia

Brunnera macrophylla

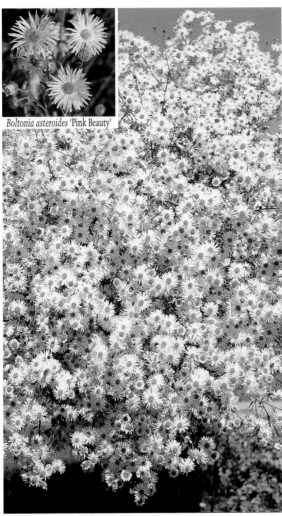

Boltonia asteroides

Boltonia asteroides 'Pink Beauty'

Brunnera macrophylla 'Variegata'

'Perfecta': lilac-red flowers and big pale purplish-brown foliage.
'Silver Light': white flowers turn pink; foliage shiny, dark green.
Zones: 3-8, heat 9-2
Spacing: 12-15" (30-45cm)
Propagation: seed, division in spring

BOLTONIA (bol-TOH-ni-a) ☼ ✄

B. asteroides (as-te-ROI-deez)
White Boltonia, Boltonia
Tall informal aster-like plant for back of borders, natural gardens. Thrives in any good garden soil; spreads rapidly in moist conditions. Vigorous plants 5-7' (1.5-2.1m) tall may need staking. Blue-green leaves. Showy daisies in late summer are white, lilac, purple or pink. Naturalized.
   'Nana': pinkish-purple flowers on mounding plants, 24-36" (60-90cm) high, spreading 24-30" (45-75cm).
   'Snowbank': white flowers, tolerates heat and humidity, height 3-4' (0.9-1.2m). Rarely needs staking when grown in full sun.

'Pink Beauty': soft pink flowers; height to about 4' (1.2m).
Zones: 4-9, heat 9-2
Spacing: 18-36" (45-90cm), more for larger species and varieties
Propagation: division, seed (species).

BRUNNERA (BROO-ne-ra) ☼ ☁ ☁ ⋙

B. macrophylla (mak-roh-FIL-a)
Heartleaf Brunnera
Fast growing perennial does well in moist and shady locations. Mid-green, heart-shaped foliage mounds 12-18" (30-45cm) high. Loose, branching clusters of pale forget-me-not blue blossoms in spring.
   'Variegata': green leaves with broad white margins.
Zones: 3-8, heat 9-3
Spacing: 12-15" (30-38cm)
Propagation: seed, root cuttings, division

Trim off dead flowers to extend the season of fresh bloom for summer-flowering perennials.

BUDDLEIA (BUD-lee-a) ☀ ⛅ 🌲 ✂ 🦋

Arching, shrubby perennial, often killed to the ground in winter, is semi-evergreen to evergreen in milder climates. Prune back hard in spring. Breaks dormancy late. Showy spires of bloom open on current season's growth. Fragrant, 6-8" (15-20cm) flower clusters top leafy stems in summer. Height varies from 4' to 10' (1.2-3.0m). Attracts butterflies.

  'Black Knight': dark purple.
  'Nanho Blue': pale mauve-blue.
  'Pink Delight': pure pink.
  'White Profusion': white.
Zones: 5-10, heat 10-4
Spacing: 4-5' (1.2-.15m)
Propagation: cuttings, semi-ripe or hardwood

Buddleia 'Pink Delight'

Buddleia 'White Profusion'

Calamagrostis Xacutiflora 'Karl Foerster'

Calamintha nepeta

Caltha palustris

CALAMAGROSTIS (ka-la-ma-GROS-tis)

Reed Grass

Vigorous, upright ornamental grasses with slender stems and rough-edged leaves. Flower from summer to fall. Thrive in any fertile soil. Tolerate moist conditions; good waterside plants. Cut flower plumes fresh or dried. Remove faded tops before new growth starts in spring.
Zones: 5-9, heat 9-3
Spacing: 3-4' (0.9-1.2m)
Propagation: Division

C. Xacutiflora (a-kew-ti-FLOH-ra)
Feather Reed Grass
Robust and showy. Flower plumes rise to 5' (1.5m) or more in summer. Striking, wheat-colored seed heads persist into winter.
  'Karl Foerster' (2001 Perennial Plant of the Year): Upright habit to 5' (1.5m).
  'Stricta': Height 3-5' (0.9-1.5m).

C. arundinacea var. *brachytricha*
  (a-run-di-NAY-see-a bra-ki-TRIK-a)
Korean Reed Grass
Lower form with gracefully arching foliage. Height 24-36" (60-90cm). Flowers in fall, shimmering white or pinkish plumes. Whole plant turns buff-colored after frost. Flower heads persist into winter.

CALAMINTHA (ka-la-MIN-tha)

C. nepeta (NEP-ee-ta, ne-PEE-ta)
[*C. nepetoides* (ne-pe-TOY-deez)]
Aromatic rock garden plant is compact, mounds 12-24" (30-60cm). Tiny, rounded leaves. Pale blue to white flowers open from late summer. Good edging, herb garden plant; use leaves in herbal teas.
Zones: 5-9, heat 10-1
Spacing: 9-15" (23-38cm)
Propagation: Division, seed

CALTHA (KAL-tha)

C. palustris (pa-LUS-tris)
Marsh Marigold
Moisture-loving perennial for marshy areas and close to water. Height to 24" (60cm). Best in rich, boggy soil. Shiny green leaves. Clear yellow single or double buttercup flowers in spring. Dies back in summer; survives in dry soil when dormant. Tolerates some shade. Naturalized.
Zones: 4-9, heat 7-3
Spacing: 9-12" (23-30cm)
Propagation: seed, division

☼ = Full Sun	✂ = Cut Flowers
☁ = Partial Sun/Shade	🌲 = Evergreen
☁ = Shade	🦋 = attracts Butterflies
〰 = Groundcover	⚡ = attracts Hummingbirds

CAMPANULA (kam-PAN-ew-la)
Bellflower

Perennial bellflowers range from low-growing rock garden plants to tall border plants useful for cut flowers. All prefer moist, well-drained garden soil; apply baits to deter slugs and snails. Flowers in spring and/or summer, in white and shades of blue to pink; delicate colors develop best in partially shaded locations.
Zones: hardiness 4-10, may vary by species; heat 9-1
Spacing: 12-18" (30-45cm)
Propagation: seed, division, cuttings

C. carpatica (kar-PAT-i-ka)
Carpathian or Tussock Harebell

Low spreader for rock garden and front of border. Spreads rapidly in well-drained soil. Height 6-12" (15-30cm). Clumps of dark green foliage topped in summer by clusters of 1½-2" (4-5cm) bright blue flowers. Mulch in warmer climates to keep roots cool. Zones 3-8.
  'Blue Clips', 'White Clips': compact plants grow 6-9" (15-23cm). Big 3" (8cm) violet-blue or white flowers, light green leaves.
  'China Doll': azure-blue flowers on 9" (23cm) plants.

'Wedgewood Blue', 'Wedgewood White': violet-blue or white flowers on compact 9" (23cm) plants.

C. garganica (gar-GAH-ni-ka)
[*C. elatines* var. *garganica* (EL-a-teenz)]
Elatines Bellflower, Gargano Bellflower

Mat-forming rock garden and edging plants, 5-6" (13-15cm) tall. Leaves grayish green, kidney or heart shaped. Flowers late spring to early summer, clusters of white-eyed, pale blue star-like blossoms. Hardy only as far north as zone 5 or 6.

C. glomerata (glo-me-RAH-ta) ✂
Clustered Bellflower

Blue, purple, or white clusters of flowers top slender, 12-18" (30-45cm) plants in summer. Stoloniferous, spreads quickly in good soils.
  'Joan Elliott': more compact and branching, to 15-18" (38-45cm); deep violet-blue flowers.
  'Superba', 'Superba Alba': vigorous plants grow 20-30" (50-75cm) tall; big clusters of rich violet/white flowers; tolerates heat better than others.

Campanula carpatica 'Blue Clips'

Campanula glomerata 'Joan Elliott'

Campanula glomerata

Campanula persicifolia

Campanula poscharskyana

Canna

C. persicifolia (per-si-ki-FOH-li-a) ✂ 🌲
Peachleaf Bellflower
Medium height, 12-36" (30-90cm). Good for middle or back of border. Basal leaves evergreen in milder climates. Blue-violet flowers are bell-shaped, borne in loose clusters. Remove faded flowers to extend summer flowering season. Cultivars **'Alba'** (white) and **'Blue'** (sky-blue) both grow to about 30" (75cm).

C. poscharskyana (po-shar-skee-AH-na) 〰
Serbian Bellflower
Rapidly spreading, drought resistant bellflower for rock garden, dry wall, or edging. Blue-lilac flowers rise to 8-12" (20-30cm) in spring. Prostrate stems, kidney-shaped leaves.

C. rotundifolia (roh-tun-di-FOH-li-a)
Harebell, Bluebells-of-Scotland
Dainty, summer-flowering bellflower grows to 6-12" (15-30cm). Tolerates cold climates. Basal leaves are rounded; foliage on flowering stems is slender, grass-like. Clear blue-violet flowers.
   'Olympia': bright blue flowers; grows 12-18" (30-45cm).

CANNA (KAN-a) ☀
Canna Lily, Indian-shot
Tender perennials often planted each year in perennial or seasonal borders. Excellent for massed displays and in containers. Heights range from 18" to 5' (45cm to 1.5m). Broad, tropical-looking foliage may be bright green, bluish, or bronze. Flowers from midsummer to fall, in showy colors that range from white to shades of yellow, orange, red, and pink. For overwintering in northern zones, lift rhizomes after frost has killed tops; store in moist peat moss at 40-45°F (5-10°C).
Zones: 7-11, heat 12-1. Treat as an annual in the North.
Spacing: tall, 2-4' (0.6-1.2m);
           dwarf forms, 12-24" (30-60cm)
Propagation: division

The name Indian-shot for *Canna* is derived from the plant's hard, round, black seeds.

CAREX (KAH-reks) ☼ ☁ ☁ ⌇

C. hachijoensis 'Evergold' (ha-chi-jo-EN-sis)
[*C. morrowii* 'Variegata' (mo-ROH-ee-y)]
Silver Variegated Japanese Sedge
Easy to grow semi-evergreen grass forms neatly rounded clusters 12-18" (30-45cm) across and 12" (30cm) high. Useful as edging or solitary plants. Gracefully curving leaves striped green, gold and white.
Zones: 5-9, heat 12-1
Spacing: 12-24" (30-60cm)
Propagation: division

CARYOPTERIS (ka-ree-OP-te-ris) ☼ 🦋

C. Xclandonensis (klan-doh-NEN-sis)
Woody perennial develops flower clusters in leaf axils on current year's growth. For more blossom, cut out flowered stems. Border and accent plant. Grows 3-4' (0.9-1.2m) high. Intolerant of cold wet soils.
  'Dark Knight': dark blue flowers, silvery green leaves. Grows 18-30" (45-60cm) tall.
  'Longwood Blue': sky-blue flowers and silver foliage on 18-24" (45-60cm) plants.
Zones: 5-9, heat 9-2
Spacing: 36-48" (90-120cm)
Propagation: cuttings

CATANANCHE (ka-ta-NAN-kee) ☼ ❧ 🦋

Cupid's-dart
C. caerulea (se-REW-lee-a)
Blue Cupid's-dart
Upright border perennial grows 18-30" (45-75cm). Best in fertile, well-drained soil. Summer flowers on wiry stems above narrow, gray-green leaves. Good in fresh or dried arrangements. Cultivars offer white and shades of blue. Damp soil may result in winter kill.
Zones: 4-10
Spacing: 9-12" (23-30cm)
Propagation: division in spring; root cuttings in fall

Caryopteris X*clandonensis* 'Dark Knight'

Caryopteris X*clandonensis* 'Longwood Blue'

Carex hachijoensis 'Evergold'

Catananche caerulea

Centaurea macrocephala

CENTAUREA (sen-TAW-ree-a) ☼ ✄ 🦋

Knapweed, Cornflower

Perennial cornflowers grow best in well-drained soil. Good in borders and for cutting.

Zones: 3-8, heat 9-1
Spacing: 12-18" (30-45cm)
Propagation: division, seed

C. dealbata (dee-al-BAY-ta)

Persian Cornflower

Late spring flowering, grows 18-30" (45-75cm) tall. Leaves coarsely cut, may grow to 24" (60cm). Deeply fringed lavender flowers 2-3" (5-8cm) across.

C. macrocephala (mak-roh-KEF-a-la)

Globe Centaurea

Flowers in summer on 3-4' (0.9-1.2m) plants. Deep green leaves have wavy margins. Yellow, globe-like flowers, 3-4" (8-10cm) across.

C. montana (mon-TAH-na)

Mountain Bluet

Early summer flowers on spreading plants, 18-24" (45-60cm) tall. Best when grown in alkaline soils. Foliage silvery when young. Flowers are deep cornflower-blue.

CENTRANTHUS (sen-TRAN-thus)

C. ruber (ROO-ber) ☼ ☁ ✄ 🦋

Red Valerian

Vigorous, dependable perennial thrives in infertile, alkaline, well-drained soils. Height 18-36" (45-90cm). Useful in borders and for cutting. Blue-green leaves. Showy clusters of small carmine-red fragrant flowers, late spring to summer; cultivars are white and shades of red and rose. Cutting stimulates continued flower production.

Zones: 4-8, heat 9-2
Spacing: 18-24" (45-60cm)
Propagation: seed, division

> After digging the flower bed to loosen the ground and to mix in added fertilizer and soil amendments, rake the surface so the soil is uniform and level before planting.

Centaurea montana

Centranthus ruber

CERASTIUM (se-RAS-ti-um) ☀ ⋙ ♠
C. tomentosum (toh-men-TOH-sum)
Snow-in-summer
Useful creeper for rock gardens, walls, edging. Spreads rapidly in northern zones; burns out in southern heat. Needs excellent drainage. Silvery leaves form blanket mounding 6-8" (15-20cm). Bright white small yet showy flowers, late spring and early summer. Remove faded flowers to stimulate new growth. Fertilize sparingly to contain vigor.
Zones: 2-7
Spacing: 12-24" (30-60cm)
Propagation: seed, division

Cerastium tomentosum

Ceratostigma plumbaginoides

CERATOSTIGMA (se-ra-toh-STIG-ma)
C. plumbaginoides (plum-ba-ji-NOI-deez)
[Plumbago larpentiae ☀ ☁ ⋙ ♥
(plum-BAH-goh lar-PEN-tee-ay)]
Leadwort
Vigorous spreading mounds of shiny leaves thrive in almost any well-drained garden soil. Useful as edging, groundcover, or rock garden plant. Height 8-12" (20-30cm). Foliage opens late in spring, turns bronze red in fall. Flowers deep gentian blue, from late summer to early fall. Provide winter protection in northern zones.
Zones: 5-9, heat 8-1
Spacing: 18-24" (45-60cm)
Propagation: division in spring

Chamaemelum nobile

Chelone lyonii

CHAMAEMELUM (ka-mee-MAY-lum)
C. nobile (NOH-bi-lee)
[*Anthemis nobilis* (AN-the-mis NOH-bi-lis)]
Roman Chamomile
Low evergreen groundcover or lawn substitute forms soft gray-green mat about 4" (10cm) thick. Spreads rapidly in well-drained soils; tolerates drought. Flowers from late spring; white daisy-like blossoms rise to 12-14" (30-35cm). Trim or mow off flowers to maintain groundcover. Blossoms used in tea; oil has flavoring and softening qualities.
   'Treneague': less vigorous and no flowers: needs less trimming and mowing.
Zones: 4-8, heat 12-1
Spacing: 12-18" (15-45cm), more closely for faster cover
Propagation: seed, division

> For eye-catching floral displays, plant smaller perennials and annuals in clusters or drifts. Larger areas viewed from some distance will need proportionately bigger groupings and massed plantings.

CHELONE (ke-LOH-nee)
C. lyonii (ly-OH-nee-y)
Pink Turtlehead
Unusual perennial for moist rich soils and wet areas. Best in acid conditions; tolerates some alkalinity. Height 24-36" (60-90cm). Leaves dark green. Dense spikes of rose-pink flowers for about four weeks in summer. For fuller growth, pinch tips when spring shoots are about 6-9" (15-23cm) long. Tolerates full sun in the North. Naturalized.
Zones: 3-8, heat 9-3
Spacing: 15-18" (38-45cm)
Propagation: division, seed

> Remove dead flowers from herbaceous and bedding plants unless seed is required. Possible sites of infection are removed along with the dead and dying tissues, and, at the same time, plant energy is directed to further flower production. Spike flowers like those of delphinium need not be cut right to the ground, since lateral growth on the same stem often flowers later.

CHRYSANTHEMUM (kri-SAN-the-mum)
Chrysanthemum, Daisies, Mums

Group of showy and reliable hardy perennials for borders and massed plantings. Best grown in fertile well-drained soil. Leaf shapes vary; foliage often aromatic. Flowers in all colors except blue, with many forms from daisy to full cushion. Long-lasting when cut. Cut tops to the ground after killing frost in fall, and apply winter mulch in cold areas. When new spring shoots are 6-8" (15-20cm) long, pinch tips to encourage bushiness. Divide in spring every 2-3 years.

Zones: 4-10, heat 12-1
Spacing: 18-30" (45-75cm)
Propagation: division, seed

C. coccineum, Pyrethrum, Painted Daisy,
see *Tanacetum coccineum* page 157

C. Xmorifolium (mo-ri-FOH-li-um)
[*Dendranthema* X*grandiflorum* (den-DRAN-the-ma)]
Chrysanthemum, Garden Mum

Diverse group of colorful perennials for fall displays. Early, midseason and late developing varieties provide color from late summer to freeze. Height 1-5' (0.3-1.5m); taller varieties need support. Leaves usually lobed and dark green or gray-green. To encourage branching, pinch shoot tips when 6-8" (15-20cm). Repeat pinching for later flowering varieties as needed until early summer when flower buds form. Most varieties spread 24-30" (60-75cm). Zones 5-10.

Many cultivars, usually grouped by flower form and plant habit:

Cushion: Double flower form; compact to 20" (50cm) or less.
Daisies: Single, yellow-centered daisies; cultivar heights vary.
Decorative: Taller plants with double or semi-double flowers, larger than those of cushion types.
Pompon: Free-flowering varieties with small, ball-shaped blossoms; usually less than 18" (45cm) tall.
Button: Small double flowers are less than 1" (2.5cm) across; usually less than 18" (45cm) tall.

C. pacificum, Silver-and-gold Chrysanthemum,
see *Ajania pacifica* page 30

C. parthenium, Feverfew, Matricaria,
see *Tanacetum parthenium* page 157

C. Xrubellum (roo-BEL-um)
[*Dendranthema zawadskii* (zah-WARD-skee-y)]
Hybrid Red Chrysanthemum

Compact and branching, masses of daisy-like flowers in late summer. Height 24-36" (60-90cm). Leaves 4" (10cm) long, deeply lobed. Fragrant flowers are 2-3" (5-8cm) across, pink to rosy-red. Zones 5-9.

'Clara Curtis': deep pink daisies with raised yellow centers.

C. Xsuperbum, Shasta Daisy,
see *Leucanthemum Xsuperbum* page 110

Chrysanthemum Xmorifolium

Chrysanthemum X morifolium

Chrysanthemum X morifolium

Chrysanthemum X morifolium

Chrysanthemum X morifolium

Chrysanthemum X morifolium

Chrysanthemum X morifolium

Chrysanthemum X morifolium

Chrysanthemum X morifolium

Chrysanthemum X rubellum

CHRYSOGONUM (kri-SOG-o-num)
Goldenstar, Green-and-Gold
C. virginianum (vir-ji-nee-AH-num)
Green-and-gold
Low mat-forming plant with bright yellow blossoms from spring to early summer, longer in northern zones. Height 6-9" (15-23cm). Best in rich, moist, well-drained soil. Good for rock garden, edging, and woodland plantings. Tolerates full sun with adequate moisture; needs at least afternoon shade in warmer climates.
Zones: 5-9
Spacing: 12-15" (30-45cm)
Propagation: seed, division

CIMICIFUGA (si-mi-si-FEW-ga)
Bugbane
Tall, slender woodland plants for shaded locations with rich, moist soil. Divided foliage makes attractive, airy mound beneath blossoms. Long, slender racemes of fragrant white flowers in summer or fall.
Zones: 3-9, heat 12-1
Spacing: 10-12" (25-30cm)
Propagation: seed, division

C. americana (a-me-ri-KAH-na)
American Bugbane, Rattletop, Summer Cohosh
Late summer flowers on 3-4' (0.9-1.2m) plants. Naturalized.

C. racemosa (ra-se-MOH-sa)
Snakeroot, Cohosh Bugbane
Late summer flowers rise on branching stems to 6-8' (1.8-2.4m), persist for about 4 weeks. Best with constant supply of moisture. Naturalized.

C. ramosa 'Hillside Black Beauty' (PP09988) (ra-MOH-sa)
Black Snakeroot
Fragrant, blush-tinted white flowers in mid- to late fall. Purplish foliage.

C. simplex (SIM-pleks)
Kamchatka Bugbane
Flowers in late fall on arching stems. Height 3-4' (0.9-1.2m).

Perennials whose bushy or tall growth is likely to sprawl or flop over, especially in windy locations, need added support as they grow. Small twiggy branches can be placed around or among the new young growth of asters, phlox, and similar bushy habit plants; flowers can then grow upright through the supports. Use individual canes or light stakes for flower stems of delphinium, lupine, and hollyhock *(Alcea)*, adding non-restrictive ties as stems grow so each one is tied in several places.

Chrysogonum virginianum

Cimicifuga ramosa 'Hillside Black Beauty'

Cimicifuga simplex

CLEMATIS (KLEM-a-tis)

Clematis, Virgin's-bower

Showy, large-flowered vine for use on wall, trellis or post. Thrives where roots can be kept cool with shade, mulch, or other plants. Best in alkaline or limestone soil with consistent moisture. Leafstems often curl like tendrils. Flowers open 6" (15cm) or more across, have colorful petaloid sepals and contrasting stamens. Most hybrids climb 8-12' (2.4-3.6m) high. Many need little pruning except to remove dead or unwanted growth.

Zones: 4-8, heat 9-1
Spacing: 4' (1.2m)
Propagation: stem cuttings

Clematis hybrids and cultivars:

'**Comtesse de Bouchard':** profuse rosy lilac-pink, satiny flowers from summer to early fall; vigorous: prune hard in early spring.

'**Duchess of Edinburgh':** double white rosette-shaped flowers in early summer and again in fall.

'**Elsa Spath':** large rich lavender-blue flowers, from summer to early fall.

'**Ernest Markham':** petunia-red flowers, late summer to fall; robust vine grows 12-16' (3.6-4.8m); prune hard in early spring.

'**Hagley Hybrid':** profuse shell-pink flowers from summer to early fall; grows 6-8' (1.8-2.4m); prune hard in early spring.

'**Henryi'** (HEN-ree-y): large white flowers, summer to early fall.

'**Jackmanii'** (jak-MAN-ee-y): profuse deep purple flowers from summer to early fall; prune hard in early spring.

'**Nelly Moser':** light mauve sepals with stronger pink center bands; profuse extra-large flowers in early summer, again in fall.

'**Ramona':** large clear blue, dark-centered flowers throughout summer. Vigorous vine grows 10-16' (3.0-4.8m).

'**The President':** large dark blue to reddish plum flowers with paler center bands and silvery reverse to sepals; resists fading; flowers continually from early summer through fall.

'**Ville de Lyon':** red flowers with golden centers from summer to early fall; prune hard in early spring.

C. integrifolia (in-teg-ri-FOH-li-a)

Solitary Clematis

Upright to spreading vine for ground, low supports, shrubs. Mounds 2-4' (60-90cm). Undivided 4" (10cm) leaves. Single, bell-like, blue-purple flowers open in midsummer on stem tips. Hardy to zone 3.

C. recta (REK-ta)

Ground Clematis

Rambling, spreading creeper mounds to about 4' (1.2m). Grows well over low supporting twigs or shrubs. Leaflets 1-2" (2.5-5m). Clouds of fragrant white flowers in midsummer. Hardy to zone 3.

'**Purpurea':** reddish-purple foliage.

C. terniflora (ter-ni-FLOH-ra)

[*C. paniculata* (pa-ni-kew-LAH-ta)]

Sweet Autumn Clematis

Fragrant and reliable vine or creeper has profuse white blossoms from late summer to fall. Stems grow 10-20' (3.0-6.0m) long.

Clematis 'Nelly Moser'

Clematis 'Ernest Markham'

Clematis 'General Sikorsky'

Clematis 'Jackmanii'

Clematis 'Lady Betty Balfour'

Clematis languinosa 'Candida'

Clematis 'Multi-Blue'

Clematis 'Ramona'

Clematis 'Ville de Lyon'

Clematis alpina 'Frances Rivis'

Clematis montana 'Tetrarose'

Clematis tangutica

Clematis terniflora

CONVALLARIA (kon-va-LAH-ri-a)
C. majalis (ma-JAH-lis)
Lily-of-the-valley
Spreading, low-growing perennial with deep green foliage, delightfully fragrant flowers in spring. Prefers rich, moist soil; tolerates dry soil in shade. Leaves to 8" (20cm). Five to eight white, bell-like flowers hang from each arched stem. Height to 12" (30 cm).
Zones: 2-8, heat 9-1
Spacing: 8-12" (20-30cm)
Propagation: division of fleshy underground stems

> Some hybrid clematis flower best when pruned hard, close to the ground, in spring; others do not need such treatment. The difference is in the age at which shoots flower. Late summer flowering varieties, such as 'Jackmannii' and its derivatives, flower on current season's growth, and are encouraged by hard pruning. Earlier blooming clematis, like 'Nelly Moser', flower on shoots that grew during the previous season. These varieties should be pruned only as necessary to shape the vines.

COREOPSIS (ko-ree-OP-sis)
Coreopsis, Tickseed
Brilliant daisy-like flowers in spring or summer, for natural and filler plantings and for cutting. Best in well-drained soil. Remove faded flowers and stems to encourage continuous blooming. Naturalized.
Zones: 3-9, heat 12-1
Spacing: 10-20" (25-50cm)
Propagation: division, seed

C. 'Tequila Sunrise' (PP9875)
Hybrid coreopsis with yellow-orange blossoms and variegated foliage. Leaves are olive green with cream and yellow markings.

C. auriculata (aw-ri-kew-LAH-ta)
Mouse Ear Coreopsis
Spring flowers golden-yellow, 1-2" (2.5-5.0cm) across. Height 12-24" (30-60cm). Spreads slowly. Provide consistent moisture to avoid early dormancy. Leaves dark green.
  'Nana': bright orange-yellow flowers. Height to 9" (23cm); great for rock garden or edging.

Convallaria majalis

Coreopsis auriculata 'Nana'

Coreopsis 'Tequila Sunrise' (PP9875)

Coreopsis grandiflora

Coreopsis rosea

Coreopsis verticillata 'Zagreb'

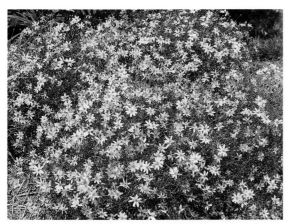

Coreopsis verticillata 'Moonbeam'

Coronilla varia

C. grandiflora (gran-di-FLOH-ra)
Coreopsis, Tickseed
Summer flowers are orange to yellow, single, semi-double, or double, 1-3" (2.5-8cm) across. Height 12-24" (30-60cm). Upper leaves deeply lobed, lower ones simple.
    'Sunray': double and semi-double golden yellow flowers on 18-24" (45-60cm) plants.

C. lanceolata (lan-see-oh-LAH-ta)
Lance Coreopsis
Summer-flowering, bushy plants to 24" (60cm). Bright yellow flowers. Lance-shaped leaves on flowering stems.
    'Goldfink': single yellow flowers with orange centers; height to 10" (25cm).

C. rosea (ROH-zee-a)
Rose Coreopsis
Late summer flowers have pink-purple petals with yellow centers. Height 9-15" (23-38cm). Spreading habit; prefers moist conditions.

C. verticillata (ver-ti-si-LAH-ta)
Threadleaf Coreopsis
Summer flowering coreopsis with single clear yellow blossoms. Height 18-36" (45-90cm). Foliage divided, fern-like. Drought tolerant.
    'Grandiflora' ('Golden Showers'): bright yellow 2 1/2" (5cm) flowers on 18-24" (45-60cm) plants.
    'Moonbeam' (1992 Perennial Plant of the Year): prolific, soft muted-yellow flowers cover plants early summer to fall. Grows 18-24" (45-60cm).
    'Zagreb': deeper yellow flowers on compact, upright plants that grow 8-18" (20-45cm) high.

CORONILLA (ko-roh-NIL-a) ☀ ☁ 〰
C. varia (VAR-i-a)
Crown Vetch
Reliable and vigorous spreader, useful for erosion control on banks and as filler in large-scale plantings. Grows in any well-drained garden soil. Height 18-24" (45-60cm). Foliage compound. Flowers in clusters, pink or pinkish-white, from early summer until frost.
Zones: 3-10
Spacing: 36" (90cm)
Propagation: seed, division

CORTADERIA (kor-ta-DEE-ri-a) ☼ ✄
C. selloana (se-loh-AH-na)
Pampas Grass
Giant clump-forming ornamental grass, useful for accent, background, or screen. Prefers fertile, well-drained soil; must have good winter drainage. Tolerates intermittent drought. Huge flower plumes, in silvery white or pink, on stems up to 12' (3.6m) tall. Cut top growth back in late winter.
Zones: 7-9, heat 12-7
Spacing: 2-4' (0.6-1.2m)
Propagation: division

CORYDALIS (ko-RID-a-lis) ☁ ☁
Low, clumping perennials for edging, front of border, rock garden. Foliage bluish green and fern-like, persisting (may be brown-green) in mild winters. Best where drainage is excellent.
Zones: 5-7, heat 8-3
Spacing: 8-10" (20-25cm)
Propagation: seed, division in spring

C. flexuosa (fleks-ew-OH-sa)
China Blue Corydalis
Showy clusters of blue flowers open in early summer. Plants often become dormant in summer and rebloom in fall. Zones 5-8.

C. lutea (LOO-tee-a)
Yellow Corydalis
Height 9-15" (23-38cm). Small, golden yellow flowers in spring. Tolerates alkaline soils.

CRAMBE (KRAM-bee) ☼ ☁
Big clusters of tiny, fragrant white flowers rise above mounds of rounded foliage. Good for borders, wild gardens, in well-drained neutral to alkaline soil. Shelter from strong winds; grow with some shade in southern areas.
Zones: 5-9, heat 9-6
Spacing: 30-40" (75-100cm)
Propagation: seed, root cuttings, division

C. cordifolia (kor-di-FOH-li-a)
Colewort
Early summer flower clusters reach 3-4' (0.9-1.2m) across and 5' (1.5m) high. Leaves green, 6-12" (15-30cm) in diameter, form mounds spreading 3-3½' (0.9-1.05m). Cut back fading leaves in late summer.

C. maritima (ma-RIT-i-ma)
Sea Kale
Smooth, fleshy, rounded gray leaves on thick purplish stems. Small, white, honey-scented flowers borne in close clusters. Height to 30" (75cm). Tolerates coastal climates. Young, blanched stems edible (late winter and spring).

Cortaderia selloana

Corydalis lutea

Crambe cordifolia

Crocosmia X*crocosmiiflora*

Crocosmia X*crocosmiiflora* 'Lucifer'

Dahlia species

CROCOSMIA (kroh-KOZ-mi-a)

C. Xcrocosmiiflora (kroh-koz-mee-y-FLOH-ra)
Crocosmia, Montbretia

Free-flowering corm plant with brilliant colors. Useful addition to perennial plantings. Prefers moist yet well-drained soil. Height 24-36" (60-90cm). Long, stiff leaves contrast well with other foliage in mixed plantings. Flowers in mid- to late summer for about four weeks. Excellent cut flower. Grow in a sheltered location north of zone 7, or lift corms each fall and replant in spring.

  'Emily McKenzie': bright orange flowers with crimson throats, on 24-30" (60-75cm) stems.

  'Lucifer': vigorous form grows to 3$^1/_2$' (1.05m); bright flame-red flowers.

  'Norwich Canary': late-flowering, vivid yellow-orange flowers, 24-30" (60-75cm) tall.

Zones: 5-9, heat 9-2
Spacing: plant corms 3" (8cm) deep, 6" (15cm) apart.
Propagation: division, removal of offsets from corms

DAHLIA (DAHL-ya)

Tender perennials often planted each year for colorful massed displays or individual settings. Smaller hybrids useful in containers. Vigorous development in spring and early summer result in brilliant blooms from mid-summer to frost. Excellent cut flowers; many forms. Dahlias perform well in any good garden soil with consistent water supply. Heights range from 12" (30cm) to 8' (2.4m), with blossom diameters from less than 1" (2.5cm) to 18" (45cm). Taller plants need support. For overwintering, lift tuberous roots after first frost; treat with fungicide to minimize rotting; store in moist sand or peat moss at 40-45°F (5-10°C). Check tubers for rot and moisture need occasionally during winter months.

Zones: 8-10 (treat as annual in the North); heat 9-3
Spacing: 15-30" (38-75cm)
Propagation: division of tubers before replanting in spring

DELPHINIUM (del-FIN-i-um) ☼ ⚘ 🦋 🐦

Delphinium, Larkspur

Colorful, elegant flower spikes rise above clumps of divided lobed foliage. Best in deep, fertile, well-drained, neutral to alkaline soil. Excellent background or accent in temperate zones. Many shades of blue, lavender, purple, and pink as well as white, yellow, and red. Taller plants need staking; flower stems tend to be hollow and brittle. Trim off fading flowers to encourage more blossom from lower side stems. When leaves yellow, cut stems back to plant base so new shoots can grow for fall flowering. Often short-lived, especially in warmer climates; easy to grow from seed.

Note: plant juices known to poison cattle.

Zones: 3-7, heat 6-1
Spacing: 24-36" (60-90cm)
Propagation: seed, division, stem cuttings

D. cardinale (kar-di-NAH-lee)

Scarlet Larkspur

Short-lived perennial hardy in zones 8-9. Height 2-5' (0.6-1.5m). Leaves finely divided. Scarlet flowers have long yellowish spurs.

D. elatum hybrids (e-LAH-tum)

Bee Delphinium

Summer flowering, single or double flowers in shades of blue or purple, white or pink. Height varies, 2-8' (0.6-2.4m).

Pacific Hybrids: tall showy flower spikes; good for background, tall accent. Short-lived.

Connecticut Yankee Series: shorter, much-branched flower stems grow to 30" (75cm).

Selection **'Blue Fountains'** reliable in zone 8.

Belladonna Hybrids [*D.* X*belladonna*]: compact, branching flower stems rise 3-4' (0.9-1.2m); flowers blue or white.

New Millennium Series, New Zealand Hybrids: strong stems with fully double flowers rising to 5-6' (1.5-1.8m). Improved tolerance of heat and humidity; moderately long-lived.

Pennant: mixed colors with wide range from rose and creamy shades to lavender and blue. Height 24-28" (60-70cm).

Round Table Mixed: Tall, stately spires of white, pink, lavender, blue, and purple. Grows to 6' (1.8m).

Delphinium elatum 'Belladonna'

Delphinium grandiflorum

Delphinium elatum Round Table Mixed

Dennstaedtia punctiloba

Delphinium elatum

Deschampsia caespitosa

D. grandiflorum (gran-di-FLOH-rum)
Chinese Delphinium
Summer-flowering species with blue or white blossoms on 24-36" (60-90cm) stems. Good middle or front of border accent. Blooms all summer when plants are cut back regularly.

DENDRANTHEMA (den-DRAN-the-ma)
see *Chrysanthemum* page 62

DENNSTAEDTIA (den-STET-i-a)
D. punctiloba (punk-ti-LOH-ba)
Hay-scented Fern
Deciduous, vigorously spreading fern grows 10-12" (25-30cm) high. Pale green, finely cut fronds are sweetly fragrant when crushed. Fall color light red-brown. Grows well in wide variety of soils. Tolerates drought. Useful on rocky slopes, under trees, on barren ground.
Zones: 3-8, heat 8-1
Spacing: 18-24" (45-60cm)
Propagation: division

DESCHAMPSIA (dez-KAMP-si-a)
D. caespitosa (sez-pi-TOH-sa)
Tufted Hair Grass
Dense clumps of dark green leaves form mounds 24-36" (60-90cm) high. Flowers in summer on erect stems; large, lacy clusters (panicles) have silvery-green or golden-green to purple coloring. Native of boggy soils; tolerates moist conditions.
'Goldschleier': gold-tinted flowers.
Zones: 4-9
Spacing: 18-24" (45-60cm)
Propagation: division, seed

☀ = Full Sun		✂ = Cut Flowers	
⛅ = Partial Sun/Shade		🌲 = Evergreen	
☁ = Shade		🦋 = attracts Butterflies	
〰 = Groundcover		🐦 = attracts Hummingbirds	

DIANTHUS (dee-AN-thus)

Pink, Carnation

Low, clump-forming perennials and biennials flower pro-lifically in late spring and summer. Prefer slightly alka-line soil; good drainage especially important in winter. Good in rock gardens and as edging. Narrow grass-like leaves. Flowers pink, rose, red, yellow, or white.

Zones: hardiness 3-9, may vary by species; heat 9-1

Spacing: 12-18" (30-45cm)

Propagation: seed, division, layering, terminal stem cuttings

D. Xallwoodii (awl-WOOD-ee-y)

Allwood Pink, Border Carnation

Bright, colorful hybrids bloom all summer. Flowers mostly double. Foliage gray-green. Easy. Heights range 3-20" (8-50cm).

- **'Aqua':** clear white double flowers; height 10-12" (25-30cm).
- **'Doris':** compact plant with wonderfully fragrant flow-ers, salmon-pink with deep pink eye.
- **'Frosty Fire':** long-flowering with brilliant red flowers and blue-green foliage. Height 6" (15cm).
- **'Helen':** free-flowering selection in deep salmon pink.

D. barbatus (bar-BAH-tus)

Sweet William

Self-seeding biennial has flat-topped clusters of showy blossoms in late spring of second year. Best in alkaline soil. Foliage clear green. Flower petals fringed, in red, pink, white, bicolor, often with contrasting eye colors. Excellent cut flower. Plants persist 2-3 years in the South; remove fading flowers to encourage fresh new growth. Dwarf forms flower at about 6" (15cm), standard ones 9-18" (23-45cm).

D. caryophyllus (ka-ri-oh-FIL-us)

Hardy Carnation

Outdoor forms of florists' carnations have double and semi-double fragrant blossoms. Heights range 9-18" (23-45cm) and more. Foliage gray-green. Hardy to zones 6 or 7; treat as annual in colder areas.

D. deltoides (del-TOI-deez)

Maiden Pink

Low, spreading plant forms loose mat for groundcover; useful in rock garden, on wall or ledge. Height 6-12" (15-30cm). Foliage grass-like. Flowers red, pink, or rose. Tolerates partial shade.

D. gratianopolitanus

(gra-tee-ah-noh-po-li-TAH-nus)

Cheddar Pink

Compact gray-green leafy mounds grow 9-12" (23-30cm). Useful in rock garden, as groundcover and edging. Fra-grant spring flowers in shades of rose or pink; remove faded flowers to extend season.

- **'Bath's Pink':** prolific pink flowers in late spring.
- **'Fire Witch':** intense magenta pink flowers, silvery blue foliage.
- **'La Bourbille':** silvery-green foliage, clear pink single flowers.
- **'Spotty':** red-and-white flowers.
- **'Tiny Rubies':** double, deep pink flowers.

D. plumarius (ploo-MAH-ri-us)

Cottage Pink, Grass Pink

Early summer fragrant flowers rise above mounds of silver-gray leaves. Heights vary, 6-24" (15-60cm). Good for edging. Single or double flowers in reds, pinks, or white. Divide vigorous clumps every 2 to 3 years.

- **'Essex Witch':** miniature border carnation grows just 3-6" (8-15cm); rose-pink flowers with fringed petals.
- **'Spring Beauty':** fully double flowers in wide range of colors; spicy, clove-like fragrance.

Dianthus Xallwoodii

Dianthus Xallwoodii 'Aqua'

Dianthus barbatus

Dianthus caryophyllus

Dianthus gratianopolitanus 'Bath's Pink'

Dianthus plumarius 'Spring Beauty'

DICENTRA (dy-SEN-tra) ☼☁✄

Elegant plants have mounding fern-like leaves and arching sprays of heart-shaped flowers from late spring to frost. Best in fertile, light soil. Good in rock gardens, borders, near woodland. Tolerates full sun in cooler climates.
Zones: hardiness 4-9, may vary by species; heat 10-1
Spacing: 15-18" (38-45cm)
Propagation: division, root cuttings, seed

D. 'Luxuriant'
Blue-green leaves and cherry red flowers; grows to 18" (45cm) tall. Hardy to zone 3.

D. 'Zestful'
Large, deep rose flowers.

D. cucullaria (koo-kew-LAH-ri-a)
Dutchman's-breeches
Tuberous roots produce short-lived basal leaves and pinkish-white flowers in spring. Height 10-12" (25-30cm). Summer dormant. Naturalized.

D. eximia (ek-SIM-i-a) 〰
Fringed Bleeding-heart
Gray-green foliage and rose-pink flowers mound 9-18" (23-45cm). Clumps do not spread; space 8-12" (20-30cm) apart for groundcover. Naturalized. Hardy to zone 3.
   'Alba': milky-white flowers and light green foliage.
   'Bountiful': finely cut foliage; soft rosy-red flowers.
   'Snowdrift': pure white flowers.

D. formosa (for-MOH-sa) 〰
Pacific or Western Bleeding-heart
Deep pink, carmine, or white flowers in spring and summer. Gray-green foliage mounds on spreading clumps. Space 8-12" (20-30cm) apart for groundcover.

D. spectabilis (spek-TAH-bi-lis)
Bleeding-heart
Spring flowering species has rose-pink outer and white inner petals. Mounds 18-24" (45-60cm). Prefers moist, well-drained soil; in dry soil, foliage dies out before early summer. Hardy to zone 2.
   'Alba': light green foliage and white flowers.

Dicentra 'Luxuriant'

Dicentra formosa

DICENTRA

Dicentra cucullaria

Dicentra spectabilis 'Alba'

Dicentra spectabilis

Dictamnus albus

DICTAMNUS (dik-TAM-nus) ☀ ✂ 🦋
D. albus (AL-bus)
[*D. fraxinella* (frak-si-NEL-a)]
Fraxinella, Gas Plant, Dittany
Shrubby, reliable perennial for mid-border planting. Long lived; best left undisturbed in fertile, well-drained soil. Rich green, glossy, foliage has lemon odor. Aromatic white flowers in early summer. Volatile oils can sometimes be ignited. Tolerates some shade, especially in hot climates. Prefers cooler nights. Seed pods useful in dried arrangements.
   'Purpureus': pink-purple flowers, darker veins.
Zones: 3-8, heat 8-1
Spacing: 3-4' (0.9-1.2m)
Propagation: seed

DIGITALIS (di-ji-TAH-lis) ⛅ ✂ 🦋 🦅
Foxglove
Showy biennial or perennial flowers in summer. Flower spikes may be one-sided. Basal foliage forms rosette. Best in partly shaded, rich, moist, well-drained soil. Good border accent or in natural planting. Self-seeding. Tolerates sun in cooler climates. **Note:** leaves are poisonous.
Zones: 4-9, heat 10-1
Spacing: 15-24" (38-60cm)
Propagation: seed, division (perennials)

D. grandiflora (gran-di-FLOH-ra)
[*D. ambigua* (am-BIG-ew-a)]
Yellow Foxglove
Flowers creamy yellow with brown markings inside. Height 24-36" (60-90cm). Short-lived perennial or biennial. Self-seeding.

D. Xmertonensis (mer-ton-EN-sis)
Strawberry Foxglove
Large flowered form has rose to coppery blossoms on spikes 3-4' (0.9-1.2m) tall. Big velvety leaves. Tetraploid hybrid breeds true from seed. Divide plants every two years after flowering to maintain vigor.

D. purpurea (pur-PEW-ree-a)
Common or Biennial Foxglove
Purple, pink, rose, or white flowers on 4-5' (1.2-1.5m) spikes from late spring. Wrinkled, downy foliage. Biennial form, readily self-seeds in moist semi-shade.
   'Excelsior Hybrids': big flowers held upright around stem; height 5-7' (1.5-2.1m).
   'Foxy': branching habit, height to 30" (75cm).
   'Giant Shirley': height to 4' (1.2m).

Digitalis purpurea

Digitalis X*mertonensis*

DORONICUM (doh-RON-i-kum)
Leopard's-bane
D. orientale (o-ree-en-TAH-lee)
[D. cordatum (kor-DAH-tum),
    D. caucasicum (kaw-KAS-i-kum)]
Caucasian Leopard's-bane
Bright perennial for borders and early season cut flowers. Height 12-24" (30-60cm). Prefers moist, well-drained soil. Yellow daisy-like flowers in spring. Deeply toothed leaves die back in midsummer. Divide every 2-3 years to maintain vigor.
Zones: 4-9, heat 12-5
Spacing: 9-15" (23-38cm)
Propagation: division, seed

DRYOPTERIS (dree-OP-te-ris)
Wood-fern, Buckler Fern,
    Shield Fern, Male Fern
D. erythrosora (e-rith-roh-SOR-a)
Japanese Shield Fern, Copper Shield Fern, Autumn Fern
Easy to grow, vigorous evergreen fern. Fronds open rose-brown, mature glossy green. Height to 24" (60cm). Protect from cold in northern winters. Tolerates drought once established.
Zones: 5-9, heat 9-3
Spacing: 18-24" (45-60cm)
Propagation: division
Note: Check with State Department of Natural Resources for restrictions.

DUCHESNEA (dew-KES-nee-a)
D. indica (IN-di-ka)
[Fragaria indica (fra-GAH-ri-a)]
Mock Strawberry
Rapidly spreading groundcover forms mat 2-3" (5-7.5cm) thick. Grow in well-drained soil. Foliage like small strawberry leaves. Yellow flowers followed by small bitter inedible fruits.
Zones: 1-10
Spacing: 12-18" (30-45cm)
Propagation: division; new plantlets form on runners

Doronicum orientale

Dryopteris erythrosora

Duchesnea indica

Echinops ritro

Echinacea purpurea

ECHINACEA (e-ki-NAY-see-a)
Coneflower
Vigorous summer-flowering perennials. Prefer well-drained soil; must have good winter drainage. Good in borders, natural plantings. Dark green leaves with whitish hairs underneath. Daisy flowers have slightly reflexed ray petals and raised central discs. Naturalized.
Zones: 3-8, heat 12-1
Spacing: 18-24" (45-60cm)
Propagation: division, root cuttings, seed

E. angustifolia (an-goos-ti-FOH-li-a)
Narrow-leaf Coneflower
Self-seeding wildflower for natural plantings. About 24" (60cm) tall. Whitish or rose-purple flowers. Leaves 4-6" (10-15cm) long.

E. purpurea (pur-PEW-ree-a)
[*Rudbeckia purpurea* (rud-BEK-i-a)]
Purple Coneflower
Height 24-36" (60-90cm). Flowers have orange-brown raised centers and purple, rose, or white petals. Tolerates heat, drought, and wind.
  'Alba' (AL-ba): flowers creamy-white with greenish centers.
  'Bright Star': rose-colored flowers freely produced.
  'Kim's Knee High' (PPAF): low-growing, 18-24" high. Flowers clear pink, ray petals slightly reflexed. Dark green leaves.
  'Magnus' (1998 Perennial Plant of the Year) (MAG-noos): non-reflexed, rosy ray petals.

ECHINOPS (EK-i-nops)
Summer-flowering perennials with thistle-like foliage and globular flower heads that open in summer. Prefer well-drained, dry soil; tolerate drought. Good accent for center or back of border. Useful in dried arrangements: cut before flowers are fully open.
Zones: 3-8, heat 12-1
Spacing: 24-30" (60-75cm)
Propagation: root cuttings, division in spring

E. ritro (RIT-roh)
Globe Thistle
Striking globular dark blue flower heads in summer. Height 2-4' (0.6-1.2m). Foliage whitish underneath.
  'Taplow Blue': larger 2-3" (5-8cm) globes of steely blue flowers.

E. sphaerocephalus **'Arctic Glow'** (sfe-roh-KEF-a-lus)
Red-brown stems contrast with silver foliage and white flower heads. Tolerates drought. Height 24-30" (60-75cm) useful in smaller area.

ELYMUS (EL-i-mus), Wild Rye, Lyme Grass,
see *Leymus* page 111

New herbaceous perennials are planted once the soil becomes workable in early spring. Many established ones can also be lifted and divided now. If flowering has been weak through overcrowding, clumps should be divided into several pieces before replanting. The outer edges of these old clumps are often more vigorous and grow more rapidly after division than the woody centers.

Echinacea purpurea 'Alba'

EPIMEDIUM (e-pi-MEE-di-um)

Barrenwort

Compact, spreading groundcover with compound leaves and spring flowers. Best in shaded, humus-rich soils. Young foliage often tinged pink or red; fall color yellow, red, or bronze. Cut mature leaves back in spring so new growth and flower clusters can develop freely. Rhizomatous growth helps prevent soil erosion.

Zones: 4-8, heat 8-5
Spacing: 8-10" (20-25cm)
Propagation: division in late summer

E. grandiflorum (gran-di-FLOH-rum)
Longspur Barrenwort, Bishop's-hat

Mounds 8-15" (20-38cm). Bright green foliage is beige-brown in spring, bronze in autumn. Flower color red to violet to white.

E. Xyoungianum (yung-ee-AH-num)
Young's Barrenwort

Mounds 6-8" (15-20cm). Sharply serrated leaflets are tinged red in spring, deep crimson in autumn. Flowers white or rose.

'Niveum' (NI-vee-um): clear white flowers.

ERIANTHUS (e-ri-AN-thus)

E. ravennae, Ravenna Grass,
see *Saccharum ravennae* page 145

ERIGERON (e-RIJ-e-ron)

Fleabane

E. speciosus (spee-si-OH-sus)
Daisy Fleabane

Reliable border perennials grow well in sandy, relatively infertile soil that drains well. Good in rock gardens or natural plantings. Height 20-30" (50-75cm). Clusters of 1-2" (2.5-5cm) purple daisy-like flowers rise above foliage in summer. Taller plants may need staking. Cut back after flowering to stimulate new and compact growth. Naturalized.

'Azure Fairy': semi-double lavender blue flowers; grows to 30" (75cm) tall.
'Foerster's Liebling': double pink flowers, height to 18" (45cm).

Zones: 2-8, heat 8-4
Spacing: 15-18" (38-45cm)
Propagation: division

Erigeron speciosus

e

Eryngium alpinum

ERYNGIUM (e-RIN-jee-um) ☼ ✀
Sea Holly

Blue-gray plants with dense flower clusters in summer. Best in well-drained sandy soil; tolerate poor dry conditions, high salt levels. Useful accents for border, rock garden. Foliage lobed or deeply cut, spiny. Each flower head has collar of leafy bracts. Plants spread slowly, can be left undisturbed indefinitely.
Zones: 4-8, heat 8-4
Spacing: 15-21" (38-53cm)
Propagation: seed (species), division

E. alpinum (al-PY-num)
Alpine Sea Holly
Height 18-36" (45-90cm). Blue conical flower heads with soft feathery bracts. Cut off fading flowers; side branches will continue flowering.

E. amethystinum (a-me-THIS-ti-num) 🦋
Amethyst Sea Holly
Height 18-24" (45-60cm). Steely-blue flowers borne in clusters on branching stems; bracts long and spiny. Hardy to zone 3.

E. giganteum (jy-GAN-tee-um)
Giant Sea Holly
Large plants grow to 4-6' (1.2-1.8m), need wind protection. Blue flowers in big oval heads, 3-4" (8-10cm) long, with rigid, toothed bracts. Short-lived perennial best treated as a biennial. Space 36" (90cm).

ERYSIMUM (e-RIS-i-mum) ☼ ☁ ✀ 🦋
E. cheiri (KAY-ree)
[*Cheiranthus cheiri* (kay-RAN-thus)]
English Wallflower

Short-lived perennial thrives in moist, temperate climates; best grown as biennial elsewhere. Late spring flowers are fragrant and showy in yellow, gold, red, and mahogany. Especially attractive when grouped or massed in borders, containers. Height 9-18" (23-45cm). Sow seed in late summer for bloom next spring; maintain seedlings in protected area like cold frame; plant out in early spring after last hard freeze.
Zones: 5-8, heat 9-2
Spacing: 6-12" (15-30cm)
Propagation: stem cuttings, seed

Erysimum cheiri

Epimedium Xyoungianum

ERYTHRONIUM (e-rith-ROH-ni-um)
Dog-tooth Violet, Trout Lily, Fawn Lily
Small, early spring flowering tuberous perennials for natural and woodland gardens. Grow in rich, moist, well-drained soil. Pendulous flowers have reflexed petals. Summer dormant. Best in cooler climates and in neutral to acid soil. Divide well-established plants; tubers must not dry out before replanting. Naturalized.
Zones: 3-8, heat 12-7
Spacing: 6-9" (15-23cm)
Propagation: seed, offsets, division

E. albidum (AL-bi-dum)
White Dog-tooth Violet
Mottled leaves, white or pinkish flowers. Height to 12" (30cm).

E. americanum (a-me-ri-KAH-num)
Common Fawn Lily, Trout Lily
Mottled leaves, yellow flowers. Height to 12" (30cm). Hardy to zone 3.

E. grandiflorum (gran-di-FLOH-rum)
Avalanche Lily
Larger species with plain green leaves and yellow flowers. Height 12-24" (30-60cm) spread to 18" (45cm). Space 12-18" (30-45cm).

EUONYMUS (ew-ON-i-mus)
E. fortunei (for-TEW-nee-y)
Wintercreeper
Spreading, clinging woody vines make dense leafy backdrop or edging in perennial plantings, rock gardens. Grows in any good garden soil. Flowers insignificant. Susceptible to infestation by scale insects.
   'Colorata' (ko-lo-RAH-ta), Purpleleaf Wintercreeper: rambling groundcover 12-15" (30-38cm) high. Clings to porous surfaces. Foliage purplish-bronze in fall; holds color all winter.
   'Kewensis' (kew-EN-sis): small form has tiny leaves, flat, spreading stems; good in rock garden, edging. Height about 3" (8cm).
   'Variegated': small, white-edged leaves, may be tinged pink in winter; grows to 18" (45cm) high, spreads to 5' (1.5m).
Zones: 4-10, heat 9-5
Spacing: 12-24" (30-60cm)
Propagation: division, cuttings

Erythronium americanum

Euonymus fortunei 'Variegated'

Euonymus fortunei 'Colorata'

Eupatorium coelestinum

Eupatorium purpureum

Eupatorium perfoliatum

Eupatorium rugosum 'Chocolate'

Eupatorium (ew-pa-TOH-ri-um)

Boneset, Thoroughwort

Vigorous perennials with showy blossoms in late summer and fall. Prefer moist, well-drained soil. Useful in borders, natural plantings. Flower heads small, in crowded clusters. Best in full sun. Leaves coarse, pointed. Divide rapidly spreading clumps every 1-3 years. Naturalized.
Zones: see individual species for hardiness; heat 9-1
Spacing: 3-4' (0.9-1.2m)
Propagation: seed, division in spring

E. coelestinum (koy-les-TEE-num)
[*Conoclinium coelestinum* (ko-nok-LIN-ee-um)]
Hardy Ageratum, Mistflower
Grows 24-36" (60-90cm). Azure blue flat-topped flower clusters in late summer. For greater flower display, cut plants back once or twice before midsummer. Space 24-30" (60-75cm). Cultivars have white, clear blue and violet flowers. Hardy in zones 6-10.

E. perfoliatum (per-foh-li-AH-tum)
Common Boneset
White-flowered species grows naturally in moist soils. Height to 5' (1.5m). Flowers from late summer to fall. Hardy in zones 3-10.

E. purpureum (pur-PEW-ree-um)
Joe-Pye Weed
Tall and showy, needs abundant water supply or moist soil. Height 4-7' (1.2-2.1m). Big 8-12" (20-30cm) leaves emit vanilla scent when crushed. Purple flowers in fall, 12-18" (30-45cm) clusters. Zones 4-9.
  'Atropurpureum' (at-roh-pur-PEW-ree-um): purple flower stems intensify color display.

E. rugosum 'Chocolate' (roo-GOH-sum)
[*E. ageratoides*,
  Ageratiuna altissima (a-je-rah-TEE-na al-TIS-i-ma)]
White Snakeroot
White flowers open in puffy clouds from summer to fall. Chocolate-brown foliage with green/brown undersides and stems. Best with low summer temperatures. Grows 4-5' (1.2-1.5m) high. Zones 3-7.

EUPHORBIA (ew-FOR-bi-a)
Spurge

Spreading perennials with showy, colorful flower bracts. Best in well-drained soil. Plants can remain undisturbed indefinitely.

Note: milky sap can cause irritation; avoid contact with open cuts or sores.

Zones: 5-8; heat 10-2
Spacing: see individual species
Propagation: seed

E. dulcis 'Chameleon' (DUL-kis)
Purple Spurge

Upright, colorful stems with purple foliage. Flower bracts are showy yellow with tints of purple and green. Height 12-24" (30-60cm). Space 12" (30cm).

E. griffithii (gri-FITH-ee-y)
Griffith's Spurge

Numerous orange-red flower bracts in summer. Upright habit, 24-36" (60-90cm) tall. Leaves medium green with pale pink midribs. Needs constant moisture. Space 18-24" (45-60cm).

'Fireglow': more intense coloring, with orange-brown stems.

E. myrsinites (mer-si-NEE-teez)
Myrtle Euphorbia

Trailing stems clothed with gray-green foliage. Best in dry, well-drained soil, rock gardens. Yellow flower bracts in spring rise 6-9" (15-23cm). Tolerates heat well, to zone 9. Space 9-12" (23-30cm).

E. polychroma (po-li-KROH-ma)
[E. epithymoides (e-pi-ti-MOI-deez)]
Cushion Spurge

Spreading clumps grow 12-18" (30-45cm) tall. Yellow flower bracts open in early spring. Foliage pale green, turning reddish in fall. Shade from afternoon sun in hot climates. Tolerates dry soil. Forms shapely mounds; space 12-18" (30-60cm). Hardy to zone 4.

Euphorbia dulcis 'Chameleon'

Euphorbia griffithii 'Fireglow'

Euphorbia myrsinites

Euphorbia polychroma

Fallopia japonica var. *compacta*

FALLOPIA (fa-LOH-pi-a)

F. japonica* var. *compacta (ja-PON-i-ka kom-PAK-ta)
[*Polygonum japonicum* (po-LIG-o-num),
 P. cuspidatum (kus-pi-DAH-tum),
 P. reynoutria (ray-NOO-tri-a)]
Japanese Knotweed, Magic Carpet
Small form of vigorous rhizomatous spreader with
clumps that grow to 24" (60cm). Pink or pinkish-red flow-
ers. Stems hollow and jointed. Useful vigorous ground-
cover for boggy or moist places. Grow as an annual in
colder climates.
Zones: 5 or 6-9, heat 8-1
Spacing: 18-24" (45-60cm)
Propagation: seed, division

FESTUCA (fes-TOO-ka)

Fescue
Ornamental forms of turf grass grow in tufts with flat or
rolled leaf-blades. Best in light, well-drained soil with-
out added nutrients. Useful in edgings, rock gardens.
Tolerates some shade though blue-green forms develop
best color in full sun.
Zones: 4-8, heat 8-1
Spacing: 8-18" (20-45cm)
Propagation: division

F. cinerea (si-NE-ree-a) cultivars:
 'Klose': foliage dark green; mounds to 8" (20cm).
 'Solling': foliage powder-blue; mounds to 6" (15cm).

F. glauca (GLAW-ka)
[*F. ovina* var. *glauca* (oh-VY-na)]
Blue Fescue, Blue Sheep's Fescue
Silvery-blue grass has arching, slender, rolled, very fine
and soft thread-like leaves to 6" (15cm) long. Height
8-12" (20-30cm). Tufts spread only by seed. Flowers in
one-sided clusters (panicles).
 'Sea Urchin': rounded and compact; grows to 10"
 (25cm).
 'Elijah Blue': bright blue color holds well all summer,
 mounds to 10" (25cm).

F. muelleri (MEW-le-ry)
Foliage soft blue-green. Mounds to 8" (20cm).

F. tenuifolia (ten-ew-i-FOH-li-a)
Hair Fescue
Fine, velvety, yellow-green foliage on mounds 8" (20cm)
high. Spring and early summer flowers followed by deep
reddish-bronze seedheads.

Festuca glauca 'Elijah Blue'

Festuca glauca 'Sea Urchin'

FILIPENDULA (fi-li-PEN-dew-la)
Meadowsweet
Dainty summer-flowering perennials for moist locations. Best in neutral to alkaline soils. Useful in semi-shaded borders, natural plantings. Attractive lobed or divided leaves. Flowers white or pink, in foamy, loose clusters. Can remain undisturbed indefinitely.
Zones: 3-8, heat 8-1
Spacing: 24-36" (60-90cm)
Propagation: seed (species), division

F. palmata (pal-MAH-ta)
Siberian Meadowsweet
Masses of 6" (15cm) flower clusters rise above leaves. Pink color turns white as flowers mature. Height 3-4' (0.9-1.2m). Prefers very moist soil, especially in full sun.

F. rubra (ROO-bra)
Queen-of-the-prairie
Tall yet wind-tolerant. Flowers pink to peach in 6-9" (15-23cm) open clusters. Grows rapidly in boggy conditions. Height 6-8' (1.8-2.4m).
   'Venusta' (ve-NUS-ta): deeper pink flowers.

F. vulgaris (vul-GAH-ris)
[F. hexapetala (hek-sa-PET-a-la)]
Dropwort
Creamy white flowers, often tinged pink, in flattish clusters. Leaves fern-like. Height 24-36" (60-90cm). Prefers constant moisture but, having tuberous roots, tolerates drier soils than other species.
   'Flore-pleno' (FLOH-re-PLEE-noh): double flowers; grows to 24" (60cm).

FRAGARIA (fra-GAH-ri-a)
'Lipstick'
Ornamental strawberry has colorful flowers, bright green foliage and showy rose-pink blossoms that open in spring and summer. Later, a few edible fruit ripen. Plants semi-evergreen in warmer climates. Fills area rapidly; great for baskets and containers.
Zones: 3-10
Spacing: 12-24" (30-60cm)
Propagation: runners, division

Filipendula palmata

Filipendula vulgaris

Filipendula rubra

Filipenula vulgaris 'Flore-pleno'

Fragaria 'Lipstick'

GAILLARDIA (gay-LAR-di-a) ☼ ✄ 🦋
G. Xgrandiflora (gran-di-FLOH-ra)
Blanketflower

Vigorous plants for average to poor, well-drained or dry soils. Useful in borders and natural plantings in full sun. Leafy, erect, branching plants grow 24-36" (60-90cm) tall. Taller varieties may need staking. Colorful 2-4" (5-10cm) daisies in red, gold, and maroon from summer to frost. Remove faded flowers for continued display. Divide clumps every 2-3 years to prevent overcrowding. Shortlived in moist, fertile soils; intolerant of heavy wet winter conditions. Tolerates heat and drought. Naturalized hybrid of two native species.

'Baby Cole': dwarf form has red flowers banded yellow; height 6-8" (15-20cm). Space 9-12" (23-30cm).

'Burgundy': rich wine-red flowers; height 24-36" (60-90cm).

'Dazzler': golden-tipped petals have maroon centers; height to 24" (60cm).

'Goblin': dwarf form with yellow-tipped red flowers; height 9-12" (23-30cm). Space 9-12" (23-30cm).

Zones: 3-10, heat 12-1
Spacing: 18-24" (45-60cm)
Propagation: seed, division

Gaillardia Xgrandiflora 'Burgundy'

Gaillardia Xgrandiflora 'Baby Cole'

Gaillardia Xgrandiflora 'Goblin'

Gaillardia Xgrandiflora 'Dazzler'

Galeobdolon (ga-lee-OB-do-lon)
G. luteum, Golden Dead Nettle,
see *Lamium galeobdolon* page 108

Galium (GAL-i-um) ☼ ☁ ⌇
Bedstraw, Cleavers
G. odoratum (oh-do-RAH-tum)
[*Asperula odorata* (as-PER-ew-la oh-do-RAH-ta)]
Sweet Woodruff
Spreading, perennial grows 6-12" (15-30cm) tall. Good groundcover around shrubs, in borders, wooded areas. Best in moist, well-drained soils; partial shade in warmer zones. Glossy green foliage. White, starry flowers in loose clusters from spring to early summer. Stems, leaves, and flowers sweetly scented.
Zones: 4-8, heat 8-3
Spacing: 12" (30cm)
Propagation: division

Gaura (GAW-ra) ☼
G. lindheimeri (lind-HY-me-ry)
White Gaura
Clusters of 1" (2.5cm) white to rose flowers rise 3-4' (0.9-1.2m) above mounds of willow-like foliage in late spring and summer. Best in rich, well-drained soil. Useful for border, natural planting. Remove fading flowers to extend display into fall. Tolerates heat and humidity. Naturalized.
  'Siskiyou Pink': bright red-pink flowers have white stamens.
  'Whirling Butterflies': shorter habit with pure white flowers on red stems; height to 30" (75cm).
Zones: 5-9, heat 9-2
Spacing: 24-30" (60-75cm)
Propagation: seed, division

Galium odoratum

Gaura lindheimeri 'Whirling Butterflies'

Gaura lindheimeri 'Siskiyou Pink'

88

Gentiana acaulis

GENTIANA (jen-shi-AH-na) ☼ ⛅

Compact plants with open trumpet-shaped flowers in shades of blue. Need moist, humus-rich acid soil with pH 5.0-6.5. Grow in rock garden with liberal moisture and shade in warmer areas; in sheltered borders, woodland plantings and containers. Leaves form thick mat beneath flowers. Established plants best left undisturbed.
Zones: 3-7, heat 8-1
Spacing: 12-18" (30-45cm)
Propagation: seed, sown when ripe in fall, division

G. acaulis (a-KAW-lis)
Stemless Gentian
Alpine species best in cool, moist locations. Large sky-blue flowers in spring. Height to 4" (10cm).

G. septemfida (sep-TEM-fi-da)
Crested Gentian
Upright, arching stems rise 8-12" (20-30cm) high. Summer flowers dark blue. Tolerates well-drained clay soils.

HARDINESS ZONES indicate how much cold a plant can withstand while continuing to grow normally. Eleven hardiness zones are based on average annual minimum temperatures. They are stated from the coldest, zone 1 with winter temperatures of -50°F (-45°C) and colder, to the warmest, zone 11 where winters are warmer than 40°F (5°C).

HEAT ZONES indicate plant heat tolerance. They are based on the average number of days during which summer temperatures can normally be expected to rise higher than 86°F (30°C). Heat zone 12 locations average more than 210 days of potentially damaging heat, while in zone 1 that temperature is rarely exceeded for a single day. Heat zones are stated from hottest to coolest, 12-1.

☼ = Full Sun   ✂ = Cut Flowers
⛅ = Partial Sun/Shade   🌲 = Evergreen
☁ = Shade   🦋 = attracts Butterflies
〰 = Groundcover   🐦 = attracts Hummingbirds

Geranium 'Patricia'

GERANIUM (je-RAY-ni-um)
Cranesbill, Geranium
Spreading perennials with flowers in shades of mauve, blue, pink, red, and white. Good in almost any moist, well-drained soil. Distinctive lobed or dissected leaves often change color in fall. Vigorous; divide every 2-4 years. Characteristic fruits shaped like crane's beak or bill.
Zones: hardiness 4-8, may vary by species; heat 12-2
Spacing: 12-15" (30-38cm)
Propagation: division, cuttings (stem and root)

G. 'Patricia': bright pink-magenta flowers have black centers. Plants mound to 24-36" (60-90cm). Space 24-30" (60-90cm) apart.

G. Xcantabrigiense (can-ta-brig-ee-EN-see)
Long-lasting pink to rose flowers rise to 6-8" (15-20cm). Densely mounding hybrid has light green leaves. Little if any seed set. Best in zones 5-7. Space 6-8" (15-20cm). Naturalized.
  'Biokovo': White flowers have pink tint at the centers.
  'Karmina' ['Biokovo Karmina']: Strong raspberry pink flowers.

G. cinereum (si-NE-ree-um)
Grayleaf Cranesbill
Semi-evergreen, 6-12" (15-30cm) mounding plant with red or pink flowers in spring. Useful at front of border, in rock garden. Best in zones 5-7.

G. dalmaticum (dal-MAT-i-kum)
Dalmatian Cranesbill
Low growing, spreading semi-evergreen for rock garden, edging. Height 4-6" (10-15cm) taller in shade. Leaves red-orange in fall. Late spring flowers mauve or light pink. Space 6-8" (15-20cm).

G. endressii 'Wargrave Pink' (en-DRES-ee-y)
Endress's Geranium, Pyrenean Cranesbill
Salmon pink flowers carried above leafy mounds in summer. Height 15-18" (38-45cm). Glossy semi-evergreen foliage. Useful rock garden, border plant. Good drainage essential.

G. himalayense (hi-mah-lay-EN-see)
[*G. grandiflorum* (gran-di-FLOH-rum)]
Lilac Cranesbill, Lilac Geranium
Spreading clumps with 1 1/2-2" (4-5cm) violet-blue summer flowers. Height 10-15" (25-38cm). Useful for informal edging, border. Leaves bright red in fall. Best in full sun with consistent moisture.

G. macrorrhizum (mak-roh-REE-zum)
Bigroot Geranium
Semi-evergreen, spreading, rhizomatous plant forms dense leafy carpet. Height 15-18" (38-45cm). Foliage changes color in fall. Spring to summer flowers purplish-magenta. Tolerates heat. Hardy to zone 3.
  'Album' (AL-bum): white petals, pink sepals.

G. maculatum (ma-kew-LAH-tum)
Spotted Geranium, Wild Cranesbill
Self-seeding wildflower clumps grow 18-30" (45-75cm) high. Grows well in sunny, moist locations. Good for border, natural garden. Late spring flowers pinkish lilac, in clusters. Best in zones 5-8. Naturalized.

G. Xoxonianum 'Claridge Druce' (ox-oh-nee-AH-num)
Produces 2" (5cm) lilac-pink flowers all summer. Height 18" (45cm).

G. robertianum (roh-bur-tee-AH-num)
Herb Robert, Red Robin
Sprawling wild geranium rises 12-18" (30-45cm). Tiny reddish flower clusters all summer. Best in well-drained, partly shaded natural groups. Naturalized.

G. sanguineum (san-GWIN-ee-um)
Blood-red Cranesbill
Free-flowering, mounding plant grows 9-12" (23-30cm) high. Useful edging, front of borders, natural plantings. Magenta flowers in spring. Fall foliage crimson-red. Tolerates heat. Hardy to zone 3.
  'Alpenglow': compact plant has vivid rose-red flowers, dark green leaves. Height to 8" (20cm).
  'New Hampshire Purple': deep rosy-pink to purple flowers open from spring into summer. Mid-green foliage turns red-orange in fall. Height 12-18".
  G. s. var. striatum [*G. s. var. lancastriense*, **'Lancastriense'** (lan-kas-tree-EN-see)]: short, spreading form grows 4-8" (10-20cm) high. Light pink flowers with darker veins.

Geranium Xcantabrigiense 'Biokovo'

Geranium Xcantabrigiense 'Karmina'

Geranium cinereum

Geranium dalmaticum

Geranium endressii 'Wargrave Pink'

Geranium himalayense

Geranium Xoxonianum 'Claridge Druce'

Geranium sanguineum 'Alpenglow'

Geranium sanguineum var. striatum

g

GEUM (JEE-um) ☼ ⛅ ✂

Avens

Colorful spring to summer flowers with dark green compound leaves. Best with ample moisture, good drainage, and protection from hot afternoon sun. Red, orange, or yellow, single or double flowers. Remove faded flowers to extend season.

Zones: 5-7, heat 9-3
Spacing: 10-12" (20-30cm)
Propagation: division, seed

G. coccineum
[G. Xborisii (bo-RIS-ee-y)]
Boris Avens

Orange-scarlet single for front of borders, edging, or rock garden. Height 9-12" (23-30cm). Rounded, lobed foliage. Flowers late spring to early summer, then intermittently to fall. Prefers partial shade. Hardy to zone 3.

> Good drainage is essential for the majority of perennials. Roots in wet, sticky ground cannot breathe well, and the plants fail to thrive.

G. macrophyllum (mak-roh-FIL-um)
Large-leaved Geum

Spreading, rhizomatous wildflower with 1/4" (6mm) yellow flowers and big leaves. Height 12-36" (30-90cm). Prefers sandy, acid to neutral soil (pH 6.0-7.0). Space at least 12" (30cm).

G. quellyon (KEL-yon)
[G. chiloense (chil-oh-EN-see)]
Chilean Avens

Single to double spring flowers on 20-24" (50-60cm) plants. Short-lived border perennials; divide every 2-3 years to maintain vigor.

'Lady Stratheden' ['Goldball']: buttercup yellow, semi-double.

'Mrs. Bradshaw' ['Feuerball']: semi-double scarlet flowers.

G. triflorum (try-FLOH-rum)
Prairie Smoke

Rapidly spreading wildflower with distinctive plumed fruit. Prefers sandy, acid to neutral soil with pH 6.0-7.0. Unusually drooping, cream to pink flowers.

Geum quellyon

Geum coccineum

Geum quellyon 'Lady Stratheden'

Geum quellyon 'Mrs. Bradshaw'

Glyceria maxima 'Variegata'

Goniolimon tataricum

GLYCERIA (gli-SEE-ri-a) ☼
G. maxima 'Variegata' (MAK-si-ma ve-ri-e-GAH-ta)
[*G. aquatica* 'Variegata' (a-KWAT-i-ka)]
Manna Grass, Sweet Grass
Spreading ornamental grass has smoothly arched leaves, striped in green with white or creamy yellow. Height to 36" (90cm). Border or mid-size accent plant. Early spring foliage has pinkish color. Leaf-blades 2" (5cm) wide and 20" (50cm) long, arching from erect stems. Flowers in branching clusters (panicles). May become invasive.
Zones: 4-10
Spacing: 12-15" (30-38cm)
Propagation: division in spring

GONIOLIMON (gon-ee-oh-LEE-mon)
G. tataricum (ta-TAH-ri-kum) ☼ ✂
[*Limonium tataricum, L. dumosum* (li-MOH-nee-um)]
Statice, Tartarian Statice, German Statice
Clusters of white and red flowers rise 10-15" (25-38cm). Basal leaves form dense clump, spreads to 15" (38cm). Flowers useful in fresh and dried arrangements. Performs well in coastal conditions; best in moist, deep loamy soil.
Zones: 4-9
Spacing: 12-18" (30-45cm)
Propagation: seed

GYPSOPHILA (jip-SOF-i-la) ☼
Baby's Breath

Airy, graceful perennials produce profusion of tiny white or pink flowers in summer. Prefers deep, well-drained, alkaline soil (pH 7.5 or higher). Best when established clumps are left undisturbed.
Zones: 3-7, heat 9-3
Spacing: 24-36" (60-90cm)
Propagation: seed, division, cuttings

G. paniculata (pa-ni-kew-LAH-ta) ✂
Baby's-breath

Cloud-like masses of white blossoms in midsummer. Height 24-36" (60-90cm). Narrow, gray-green foliage. Cut back after first flowering to encourage fall production. Excellent for cut flowers, fresh or dried.
  'Bristol Fairy': double white flowers.
  'Perfecta': robust form has larger double white flowers.
  'Pink Fairy': smaller variety with double pink flowers; height to 18" (45cm).

G. repens (REE-penz)
Creeping Baby's-breath

Low-growing species for rock garden, edging, front of border. Forms mat 4-8" (10-20cm) deep. Gray foliage. White to lilac flowers. Space 12" (30cm).

HAKONECHLOA (ha-KOH-nee-kloh-a)
H. macra (MAY-kra)

Rhizomatous ornamental grass; height to 18" (45cm). Best in fertile, well-drained soil. Useful in borders, as accent. Soft, gracefully arching, yellow-green leaves. Flowers in late summer with delicate, open clusters (panicles). Intolerant of full sun. Spreads slowly.
  'Aureola' (aw-ree-OH-la): bright yellow leaves with fine green stripes, attractive buff color in fall.
Zones: 6-9, heat 9-2
Spacing: 12-15" (30-38cm)
Propagation: division

Gypsophila repens

Hakonechloa macra 'Aureola'

Gypsophila paniculata

Hedera helix

Helenium autumnale

HEDERA (HED-e-ra)

Ivy

Trailing woody vines that cling to porous surfaces. Grow in any good garden soil. Useful for containers, ground-cover, and cut foliage. Leaves variable. Insignificant yellowish flower clusters in fall. Dry, warm conditions encourage spider mite infestations.

Zones: 5-9, heat 12-5
Spacing: 12" (30cm)
Propagation: cuttings

H. canariensis (ka-ne-ree-EN-sis)

Algerian or Canary Ivy

Robust, warm climate vine quickly fills area. Wine-red stems; bright green foliage turns bronze-green in winter. Big leaves as wide as 5-7" (13-18cm). Hardy to zone 7. Variegated cultivars.

H. helix (HEE-liks)

English Ivy

Fine-leaved ivy with dark green foliage up to 4" (10cm) across. Many variations in size, form, leaf color.

HELENIUM (he-LEE-ni-um)

Sneezeweed

Adaptable, daisy-flowered perennial with showy orange to yellow blossoms in late summer and fall. Useful in natural plantings; stake for support in borders. Tolerates cold climates, moist soils. Naturalized.

Zones: 3-8, heat 8-1
Spacing: 18-30" (45-75cm)
Propagation: division, seed

H. autumnale (aw-tum-NAH-lee)

Common Sneezeweed, Helen's Flower

Plants grow 3-5' (0.9-1.5m). Sprays of yellow or mahogany daisies borne on dark brown-black stems. Leaves 4-6" (10-15cm) long. Several named cultivars.

H. bigelovii (bi-ge-LOH-vee-y)

Bigelow Sneezeweed

Yellow flowers have brownish-yellow central discs. Height 2-4' (1.2m).

HELIANTHEMUM (hee-li-AN-the-mum)
Sun Rose, Rock Rose ☀ 〰 🌲
H. nummularium (nu-mew-LAH-ri-um)
Common Sun Rose
Low, spreading shrubby perennial with woody stems and summer flowers. Height 6-12" (15-30cm). Best in poor, rocky or sandy, well-drained alkaline soil. Good for rock garden, dry rocky bank, edging. Dark green to gray foliage. Trim after first bloom to encourage later flowering. Cultivars have yellow, orange, red, pink, or white, single or double flowers. Need protection from severe winter temperatures.
Zones: 5-7, heat 10-3
Spacing: 18-24" (45-60cm)
Propagation: seed, cuttings

HELIANTHUS (hee-li-AN-thus) ☀ ✂
H. decapetalus (de-ka-PET-a-lus)
[*H.* ✕*multiflorus* (mul-ti-FLOH-rus)]
Thin-leaved Sunflower
Vigorous, upright perennial for back of border or natural planting. Height 3-5' (0.9-1.5m). Grows in any moist, well-drained soil. Big, oval, coarsely toothed leaves. Late summer daisy flowers yellow or yellow-orange, as big as 5" (13cm) across. Stake to support tall plants. Naturalized.
 'Flore-pleno': fully double, bright yellow flowers, 5' (1.5m) tall.
Zones: 4-8, heat 11-3
Spacing: 18-24" (45-60cm)
Propagation: seed, division

HELICTOTRICHON (he-lik-toh-TRY-kon) ☀ 🌲
Avena, Oat Grass
H. sempervirens (sem-per-VY-renz)
Blue Oat Grass, Avena
Ornamental grass with showy, blue-brown flower clusters (panicles) that rise high over arching blue-gray foliage in summer. Best in well-drained neutral to alkaline soil. Height 20-36" (50-90cm). Tolerates drought once established, and some shade.
Zones: 3-8, heat 9-1
Spacing: 12-15" (30-38cm)
Propagation: division, seed

Helianthemum nummularium

Helianthus decapetalus

Helianthemum nummularium

Helictotrichon sempervirens

Heliopsis helianthoides

Helleborus niger

Helleborus orientalis

HELIOPSIS (hee-li-OP-sis) ☼ ✄
Oxeye
H. helianthoides (hee-li-an-THOI-deez)
Sunflower Heliopsis
Showy, informal perennial for border or natural planting. Grows to 3-6' (0.9-1.8m). Best in well-drained soil. Serrated leaves 4-5" (10-13cm) long. Yellow sunflower-like blossoms in summer, 2-3" (5-8cm) across. Naturalized.
Zones: 3-9, heat 9-1
Spacing: 30-40" (75-100cm)
Propagation: seed, division

H. helianthoides subsp. *scabra* (SKAY-bra)
Rough Heliopsis
Rough, hairy foliage and fewer, orange-yellow flowers.
  '**Incomparabilis**' (in-kom-pa-RAB-i-lis): 3" (8cm) warm orange single to semi-double flowers with overlapping petals.

HELLEBORUS (he-LEB-oh-rus)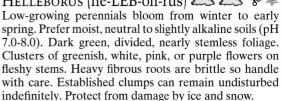
Low-growing perennials bloom from winter to early spring. Prefer moist, neutral to slightly alkaline soils (pH 7.0-8.0). Dark green, divided, nearly stemless foliage. Clusters of greenish, white, pink, or purple flowers on fleshy stems. Heavy fibrous roots are brittle so handle with care. Established clumps can remain undisturbed indefinitely. Protect from damage by ice and snow.
Note: all plant parts are poisonous.
Zones: 3-8. heat 8-1
Spacing: 12-15" (30-38cm)
Propagation: seed, division

H. niger (NY-jer)
Christmas Rose
Blooms from late fall to early spring, depending on climate. Height 12-18" (30-45cm). Cup-shaped flowers have prominent yellow stamens, are borne on red-spotted stems.

H. orientalis (o-ree-en-TAH-lis)
Lenten Rose
Winter to early spring flowers are white, pink, or purple, sometimes with darker spots. Height 15-18" (38-45cm). Leafy flower bracts.

Helleborus orientalis

HEMEROCALLIS (he-me-roh-KAL-is)
Daylily

Adaptable, low maintenance, lily-like plants with abundant summer blossoms. Flowers are single, semi-double or double with diameters ranging from 3 to 8" (8 to 20cm). Blooms are sometimes fragrant and may be ruffled or smooth.

Repeat flowering varieties provide a longer season of color.

Extended flowering blooms remain open 16 hours or more.

Nocturnal varieties open from late afternoon to evening, and remain open until next morning.

Daylilies have broad arching or grass-like leaves. Foliage is deciduous, semi-evergreen or evergreen.

Deciduous varieties are hardiest, always dying back in winter; they are also least heat tolerant and grow best in zones 3-7.

Semi-evergreens retain leaves in milder climates; apply winter mulch in colder climates; best in zones 5-9.

Evergreen varieties hold green leaves through most winters; mulch as needed to reduce cold damage; best in zones 5-9.

Cultivars with various flower and foliage characteristics are available in the range of plant sizes:

Dwarf: to 12" (30cm) high, spread 15-24" (38-60cm); space 12-24" (30-60cm) apart.

Low-growing: 12-24" (30-60cm) high, spread 18-36" (45-90cm); space 18-30" (45-75cm) apart.

Medium: 24-36" (60-90cm) high, spread 18-36" (45-90cm); space 24-36" (60-90cm) apart.

Tall: more than 36" (90cm) high, spread 30-48" (75-120cm); space 24-36" (60-90cm) apart.

All best grown in fertile, moist, well-drained soil. Tolerate heat and drought. Naturalized in many areas. Good in borders, massed for accent, smaller ones for edging and rock gardens, in natural plantings.

Zones: see foliage type above for hardiness, range 3-9; heat 12-1

Spacing: varies with plant size, as above

Propagation: division, seed (species)

Hemerocallis 'Apricot Beauty'

Hemerocallis 'Baja'

Hemerocallis 'Bonanza'

Hemerocallis 'Catherine Woodbury'

Hemerocallis 'Frans Hals'

Hemerocallis 'Happy Returns'

Hemerocallis 'Lynn Hall'

Hemerocallis 'Mardi Gras Parade'

Hemerocallis 'Rocket City'

Hemerocallis 'Siloam Byelo'

Hemerocallis 'Snowy Apparition'

Hemerocallis 'Stella D'Oro'

HERNIARIA (he-ni-AH-ri-a) ☼ ⋙ 🌲
H. glabra (GLAB-ra)
Herniary, Rupturewort
Low, moss-like creeper for rock garden, edging, between paving stones. Height to 2-4" (5-10cm). Summer flowers greenish-white. Leaves turn bronze-red in winter.
Zones: 5-9
Spacing: 10-12" (25-30cm)
Propagation: seed, division

HESPERIS (HES-pe-ris) ☼ ☁ 🦋
H. matronalis (ma-troh-NAH-lis)
Dame's-rocket, Sweet Rocket
Upright, branching, self-seeding biennial naturalized in eastern states. Height 24-36" (60-90cm). Needs consistent moisture in well-drained soil. Plant in natural garden, informal border. Leaves sharply pointed. Flowers from late spring in second year from seed: long fragrant clusters of white, mauve, or purple. Naturalized.
Zones: 3-8
Spacing: 20-30" (50-75cm)
Propagation: seed

HEUCHERA (HEW-ke-ra)
Alumroot   ☼ ☁ ✂ ⋙ 🌲 🐦
Low mounds of distinctive foliage topped by airy clusters of small, bell-like flowers in late spring and summer. Prefers rich, well-drained soil; must have good winter drainage. Mulch in winter where freezing and thawing ground can cause heaving. Tolerates stony locations. Naturalized.
Zones: 3-9, heat 8-2
Spacing: 12" (30cm)
Propagation: division, seed

H. americana (a-me-ri-KAH-na) cultivars
American Alumroot, Rock Geranium
Several cultivars with colorful foliage for light woodland or borders. Greenish or red-tinted flower clusters rise to 18-36" (45-90cm).

- **'Chocolate Ruffles':** ruffled, chocolate-colored leaves with burgundy undersides; purple flower clusters 30" (75cm) tall.
- **'Palace Purple' (1991 Perennial Plant of the Year)** [H. micrantha cv.]: deep mahogany red, ivy-form foliage fades to bronze-green in heat; flowers yellowish white, clusters rise to 12-24" (30-60cm).
- **'Pewter Veil':** new leaves coppery pink, becoming pewter silver, 6" (15cm) across; flowers rise to 15-24" (38-60cm).
- **'Plum Pudding':** plum purple foliage with silvery veins in neat, compact mound; flower on purplish spikes 15-24" (38-60cm).
- **'Ruby Veil':** slate gray, 8" (20cm) leaves are mottled with purple and ruby-red; flower height 24" (60cm).

H. Xbrizoides 'Green Ivory': profuse greenish-white flower clusters rise 30-36" (75-90cm).

H. sanguinea (san-GWIN-ee-a)
Coralbells
Mounds of heart-shaped or roundish, lobed foliage with bronze to green coloring. Flowers white to red, rising 12-24" (30-60cm). Remove faded flower stems to extend long season. Many cultivars.

Herniaria glabra

Hesperis matronalis

Heuchera americana 'Palace Purple'

Hibiscus mosceutos 'Disco Belle Series'

Hibiscus mosceutos 'Lord Baltimore'

Hibiscus mosceutos 'Turn of the Century'

HIBISCUS (hy-BIS-kus) ☼ ⛅ 🦅

Rose Mallow

H. mosceutos (mos-KEW-tos) cultivars

Fast-growing shrubby perennials have woody-based stems that survive winter in warmer climates. Showy flowers open from midsummer until chilled out in fall. Breaks dormancy late, and will grow and bloom in one season from soil level. Use for low hedge, as specimen in border, patio bed, planter. Prune to contain size. Tolerate some drought, though buds drop with very dry soil and with cold air. Grow as annual in colder climates. Naturalized.

'Anne Arundel': big pink flowers; height 4-5' (1.2-1.5m).

'Disco Belle' Series: compact habit for smaller garden, grows to 3-4' (0.9-1.2m); several colors. Space 2-3' (0.6-0.9m).

'Lady Baltimore': grows to 4' (1.2m); pink flowers have satiny red centers.

'Lord Baltimore': red flowers to 10" (25cm) across on shrub that reaches 4-5' (1.2-1.5m) each season.

'Mallow Marvels': selection of white and shades of red and pink; height 3-4' (0.9-1.2m). Space 2-3' (0.6-0.9m).

'Turn of the Century': dark red and light pink bicolor; rapid growth to 6-8' (1.8-2.4m). Space 4-5' (1.2-1.5m).

Zones: 5-9, heat 12-1

Spacing: 3-4' (0.9-1.2m)

Propagation: cuttings

Heuchera sanguinea

HOSTA (HOS-ta) ☀ ⛅ ☁ ✂ 〰

Hosta, Plantain Lily

Reliable leafy perennials with variously marked and colored foliage. Summer flower clusters are white to purple, opening close to foliage or rising above to heights of 3-6' (0.9-1.8m). Plant in moist, rich, well-drained soil. Useful for edging, low hedge, groundcover, border accent, containers, among shrubs and trees. Blue-leaf and most variegated hostas provide best color in part or full shade. Foliage heights range from 3" (7.5cm) to 36" (90cm). Clusters spread to fill space; divide as needed in fall or spring. Use bait to deter slugs and snails.

Zones: 3-9, heat 9-2
Spacing: 12-36" (30-90cm) or more; see individual varieties
Propagation: division

Hosta cultivars:

'Blue Angel': mounds 3-4' (0.9-1.2m). Big, textured, rounded to heart-shaped leaves on upright stems. White flowers rise to 4' (1.2m) in midsummer.

'Diamond Tiara': compact mounds 12-16" (30-40cm) high. Heart-shaped leaves with wide creamy-white margins. Flowers striped purple, midsummer to fall.

'Emerald Tiara': reverse 'Golden Tiara' has gold leaves edged in green. Height 12-16" (30-40cm). Flowers like 'Diamond Tiara'.

'Fair Maiden': compact 10-12" (12-15cm) mounds of variegated leaves; creamy white margins, cream on dark green base at center. Clusters of pale lavender flowers, early to midsummer.

'Fragrant Bouquet': sun-tolerant leaves have uneven wide cream margins, apple green centers. Mounds to 18" (45cm); spreads to 26" (65cm). Late summer flowers white with lavender tint.

'Francee': leaves rich green with white edges; colors hold in sun. Height 12-24" (30-60cm). Flowers lavender, midsummer.

'Ginko Craig': narrow, white-edged green leaves form neat mounds. Tall spikes of violet flowers in mid to late summer.

'Gold Standard': yellow-green leaf centers turn gold; deep green edges. Grows to 24" (60cm). Lavender flowers in midsummer.

'Golden Tiara': heart-shaped leaves with irregular gold-green margins. Compact mounds 6-12" (15-30cm) high. Flowers like 'Diamond Tiara'.

'Hadspen Blue': rounded leaves are powdery blue. Grows to 24" (60cm). Flowers in mid to late summer.

'Halcyon': heavy-textured, pointed blue leaves mound to 12" (30cm). Resists slugs well. Intense blue-lilac flowers open in mid to late summer

'June': pointed, ribbed, thick leaves have gold centers and blue-green margins. Mounds to 12" (30cm). Violet flowers in mid to late summer. Good slug resistance.

'Krossa Regal': large frosty blue foliage more upright than spreading. Mounds 24-36" (60-90cm). Flowers lavender, to 5' (1.5m) in mid to late summer.

'Moon Glow': warm golden foliage edged creamy white; color holds well. Height to 24" (60cm). White midsummer flowers.

'Northern Exposure': puckered leaves are blue-green with yellowish to cream edges. Grows 24-36" (60-90cm) high. White flowers in early to midsummer.

'Patriot': broader white margins than 'Francee'. Height to 12" (30cm); spread to 30" (75cm). Midsummer flowers pale lilac.

'Regal Splendor': creamy margins on frosty blue leaves. Mounds 24-36" (60-90cm). Lavender flowers, mid to late summer.

'Royal Standard': glossy green, spreading oval leaves. Height 18-24" (45-60cm). Pure white, fragrant flowers in late summer.

'Sagae': big, frosted green leaves have narrow creamy margins. Mounds 24-36" (60-90cm). Pale lavender flowers open in summer. Good slug resistance.

'Shade Fanfare': pale green heart-shaped leaves, creamy margins. Spreads to 30" (75cm). Lavender flowers in midsummer.

'Sum and Substance': very big (to 24", 60cm), light green leaves. Plants 3-5' (0.9-1.5m) wide, 2 1/2-3' (0.75-0.9m) tall. Lavender flowers in mid to late summer. Tolerates some sun.

'Wide Brim': big undulating dark green leaves have irregular creamy margins. Plants to 30" (75cm) across. Flowers mauve to lavender, midsummer.

***H. fortunei* 'Aureomarginata'** (aw-ree-oh-mar-ji-NAH-ta)
Dark green leaves have bright golden yellow borders. Height 12-24" (30-60cm). Flowers lilac, midsummer.

***H. kikutii* 'Kifukurin'** (ki-KEW-tee-y ki-few-KEW-rin)
Creamy yellow margins on pointed, glossy dark green leaves. Loose mound 12-24" (30-60cm) high. Clusters of lavender flowers in early to midsummer.

H. montana* forma *aureomarginata (mon-TAH-na) [*H. m.* 'Aureo-marginata']
Big pointed leaves have broad gold margins, hold color all season. Mounds 24-36" (60-90cm). Tight clusters of white flowers in summer.

***H. plantaginea* 'Aphrodite'** (plan-ta-JIN-ee-a)
Light green leaves in loose mound 12-24" (30-60cm) high. Highly fragrant, double, pure white flowers.

***H. sieboldiana* cultivars** (see-bohl-di-AH-na)
'Elegans' (EL-e-ganz): big, heavily textured blue-gray rounded leaves become distinctly corrugated with maturity. Height 24-36" (60-90cm). White flowers in compact clusters.
'Frances Williams': heavily textured blue-green leaves have broad golden yellow edges. Mounds 12-24" (30-60cm). Flowers white, early to midsummer.

***H. undulata* cultivars** (un-dew-LAH-ta)
'Albomarginata' (al-bo-mar-ji-NAH-ta): Large green leaves have broad white edges. Height 12-24" (30-60cm). Flowers white.
'Variegata' (ve-ri-e-GAH-ta) [*H. u.* 'Medio-picta' (mee-di-oh-PIK-ta)]: undulating leaves have white centers and green margins. Height 12-24" (30-60cm). Flowers lilac.

***H. ventricosa* 'Aureo-marginata'** (ven-tri-KOH-sa) [*H. v.* 'Variegata']
Gracefully uneven creamy yellow to white border on glossy deep green leaves. Mounds 12-24" (30-60cm). Flowers purple-violet.

Hosta

Hosta 'Blue Angel'

Hosta 'Emerald Tiara'

Hosta 'Francee'

Hosta 'Gold Standard'

Hosta 'Halcyon'

Hosta 'Patriot'

Hosta 'Regal Splendor'

Hosta 'Sagae'

Hosta 'Shade Fanfare'

Hosta sieboldiana 'Elegans'

Hosta undulata 'Albo Marginata'

Hosta ventricosa 'Aureo-marginata'

HOUTTUYNIA (hoo-TY-ni-a)

H. cordata (kor-DAH-ta)
Chameleon Plant
Vigorous, spreading, rhizomatous perennial for moist soils or shallow water. Useful groundcover in boggy places. Leaves heart-shaped, green. Flowers white with prominent centers.

'Chameleon' ('Camelon'): leaves marked with yellow, bronze, pink, and scarlet-red. Height 6-9" (15-23cm).

Zones: 3-8
Spacing: 12-15" (30-38cm)
Propagation: division

HYPERICUM (hy-PER-i-kum)

H. calycinum (ka-li-SEE-num)
St.-John's-wort
Spreading woody perennial has bright yellow cup-shaped summer flowers. Height 16-24" (40-60cm). Prefers well-drained soil. Useful for edging, rock garden, or sunny banks. Prostrate, rooting branches prevent soil erosion.

Foliage blue-green, purplish in fall, evergreen in warmer areas. Shear vigorous plants every few years.
Zones: 5-10, heat 9-2
Spacing: 15-24" (38-60cm)
Propagation: seed, division, cuttings

IBERIS (y-BEE-ris)

Candytuft
I. sempervirens (sem-per-VY-renz)
Evergreen Candytuft
Spreading woody perennial mounds to 9-18" (15-45cm). Best in moist, well-drained soil. Useful edging, rock garden, border plant. Narrow leaves about 1$1/2$" (4cm) long. Clusters of white flowers from late spring to early summer. Shear lightly after flowering to encourage new leafy growth. Cut woody stems back every 1-2 years.
Zones: 3-9, heat 9-1
Spacing: 12-18" (30-45cm)
Propagation: seed, division, cuttings

Houttuynia cordata 'Chameleon'

Hypericum calycinum

Iberis sempervirens

Incarvillea delavayi

Inula ensifolia

Imperata cylindrica 'Rubra'

IMPERATA (im-PER-ay-ta) ☼ ⛅ ☁
I. cylindrica 'Rubra' (si-LIN-dri-ka ROO-bra)
Japanese Blood Grass
Ornamental grass with tufts of deep red leaf blades. Best in fertile, moist yet well-drained soil. Good in borders, rock gardens. Upright, open habit, height 12-24" (30-60cm). Rhizomatous; spreads slowly.
Note: Check with State Department of Natural Resources for restrictions.
  'Red Baron': intense color holds throughout growing season.
Zones: 5-9, heat 9-4
Spacing: 15-18" (38-45cm)
Propagation: division

INCARVILLEA (in-kar-VIL-ee-a) ☼ ⛅ ✂
I. delavayi (de-la-VAY-y)
Hardy Gloxinia
Warm climate perennial with big trumpet-shaped pink flowers in early summer. Clumps mound 18-24" (45-60cm) high. Best left undisturbed in humus-rich sandy, well-drained soil. Useful in rock gardens, protected borders; select position sheltered from winter winds. Foliage deeply divided. Flowers borne in clusters. Remove faded blossoms to extend season.
Zones: 5-7
Spacing: 12-15" (30-38cm)
Propagation: seed, division

INULA (IN-ew-la) ☼ ✄ 〰
I. ensifolia (en-si-FOH-li-a)
Swordleaf Inula
Low, vigorous perennial with brilliant golden yellow daisy flowers in late summer. Height 12-24" (30-60cm). Grows in any moist, well-drained soil. Good in rock garden and at front of border. Small, lance-shaped leaves. Flowers borne singly on wiry stems. Tolerates moist soils. Divide exuberant clumps every 2-3 years.
Zones: 3-8, heat 8-1
Spacing: 12-18" (30-45cm)
Propagation: seed, division

Iris germanica

IRIS (Y-ris)
Flag, Fleur-de-lis
Spreading rhizomatous plants with sword-like leaves and distinctive, showy, colorful flowers from late spring to summer. Most prefer moist well-drained soil and tolerate periods of drought; some need constant moisture. Distinctive flowers: three petals called falls are reflexed, and three called standards turn upwards.
Zones: see individual species for hardiness; heat 8-4
Spacing: 10-18" (20-45cm)
Propagation: division

Bearded Iris, German Iris
[*I. germanica* cultivars (jer-MAN-i-ka)]
Named for the distinct beards near centers on lower petals. Colorful displays from spring to early summer and again later for reblooming varieties. Flower colors vary from solid to contrasting bicolor, in white and shades of yellow, orange, lilac, and purple. Blooms may be fragrant. Several blossoms per stem open in succession.
Bearded irises are grouped by height, with early, mid-, and late flowering forms. Foliage usually dies by late summer. Useful accents for edging, border, front of wall or shrubs, to control soil erosion on banks. Plant rhizomes at surface of well-drained soil; best with some alkalinity. Zones 3-10.
Miniature Dwarf Bearded [*I. pumila* cvs. (PEW-mi-la)]: earliest to flower, 2-3" (5-8cm) blooms rise 4-8" (10-20cm). Falls usually speckled. Best in rocky soils: must have excellent drainage.
Standard Dwarf Bearded [Lilliput]: bloom from mid-spring with 3-4" (7-10cm) flowers. Height 10-15" (25-38cm).
Intermediate Bearded: flowers open in mid to late spring. Height 15-28" (38-80cm). Sturdy stems generally need no support.
Tall Bearded: tallest and most prolific of the bearded irises. Big showy blossoms. Flowering stems taller than 28" (80cm), some rise to 48" (120cm).

I. cristata (kris-TAH-ta)
Crested Iris
Height 3-9" (8-23cm). Flowers pale lilac. Plant rhizomes at surface of well-drained soil. Good for rock garden, front of border. Zones 3-8. Naturalized.

I. ensata (en-SAH-ta)
[*I. kaempferi* (KEM-fe-ry)]
Japanese Iris
Summer-flowering irises that grow 24-36" (60-90cm) tall. Prefer slightly acid soil, moist or boggy conditions, partial shade. Useful at edge of woodland, near pond. Flowers with wide-spreading petals open to 10" (25cm) across. Selections offer single, double, peony-style flowers. Colors range from white to pink to purple to blue. Zones 4-9.

I. pallida (pa-LID-a)
Dalmatian Iris
Rhizomatous bearded iris flowers on branching stems from late spring. Fragrant, 3-5" (8-13cm) blossoms are lilac-blue with yellow beards. Zones 4-9.
  'Argentea Variegata': striped leaves are blue-green and white.
  'Aurea Variegata' ['Aurea', 'Variegata']: leaves striped green and yellow.

I. pseudacorus (soo-DAK-oh-rus)
Yellow Flag
Vigorous iris for water's edge or in soggy locations. Branching stems bear several bright yellow, dark-veined flowers to height of 6-7' (1.8-2.1m). Cultivars offer variety of bloom color. Zones 4-8.

I. sibirica (si-BI-ri-ka)
Siberian Iris
Summer flowers in shades of blue or white. Height 24-36" (60-90cm). Prefer slightly acid soil, moist or boggy conditions, partial shade. Useful at edge of woodland, near pond. Tolerate drier conditions if watered during growing season. Divide clumps when flower production fails. Zones 3-9.

I. versicolor (ver-SIK-o-lor)
Wild Iris, Wild Flag
Selfseeding wildflower of wet soils. Prefers slightly acid soil, moist or boggy conditions, partial shade. Use at edge of woodland, near pond. Naturalized.
Note: rhizome juices may cause dermatitis.

Iris pumila

Iris cristata

Iris ensata

Iris pallida

Iris pseudacorus

Iris sibirica

KALIMERIS (ka-LIM-e-ris) ☼ ☁
K. pinnatifida (pi-na-TIF-i-da)
[*Asteromoea mongolica* (as-te-ROH-mee-a mon-GOL-i-ka), *Boltonia indica* (bol-TOH-ni-a IN-di-ka)]
Double Japanese Aster
Boltonia relative grows 18-30" (45-75cm) tall, thrives in any good garden soil that drains well. Lower leaves 2-4" (5-10cm) long; upper leaves small, light green. Loose clusters of small, semi-double, white daisies with pale yellow centers open throughout summer.
Zones: 3-8
Spacing: 24-30" (60-75cm)
Propagation: division

KNAUTIA (NOW-tee-a) ☼ ✄
K. macedonica (ma-se-DON-i-ka)
Easily grown bushy perennial with dark red scabious-like flowers. Lacy foliage contrasts with pincushion blooms on branched stems. Height 18-24" (45-60cm) high, spread to 24" (60cm). Good for informal borders, to naturalize. Useful cut flower, fresh dried designs. Plant in well-drained neutral or slightly alkaline soil. Unusual color.
Zones: 4-8
Spacing: 20-24" (50-60cm)
Propagation: seed, division
Note: Check with State Department of Natural Resources for restrictions.

Kalimeris pinnatifida

Knautia macedonica

KNIPHOFIA (ny-FOH-fi-a) ☼ ☁ ✄ ⚹
Torch Lily, Poker Plant, Tritoma
K. uvaria (oo-VAH-ri-a)
Red-hot Poker, Common Torch Lily
Poker-like flower clusters rise in summer from clumps of long, narrow, gray-green leaves. Height 3-5' (0.9-1.5m). Grow in well-drained garden soil. Flower color red, orange-red, yellow, coral, or cream. Plant no deeper than 2-3" (5-8cm). For winter, remove flower stems; tie leaves together to protect crown; and mulch with dry material to keep moisture out, prevent freezing and heaving. Or lift crown each fall and store through winter in cool moist sand. Divide older clumps.
Zones: 5-9, heat 9-1
Spacing: 3-4' (0.9-1.2m)
Propagation: seed, division, offsets

LAMIUM (LAY-mi-um) ☼ ☁ ☁ ⌇
Dead Nettle
Spreading stoloniferous perennials grow 8-24" (30-60cm) high. Thrive in any well-drained soil. Useful especially in shade for groundcover, containers, to naturalize. Vigorous growth; may become invasive.
Zones: 3-8, heat 8-1
Spacing: 15-18" (38-45cm)
Propagation: seed, division

L. galeobdolon (ga-lee-OB-do-lon)
[*Galeobdolon luteum* (LOO-tee-um), *Lamiastrum galeobdolon* (la-mi-AS-trum)]
Golden Deadnettle, Yellow Archangel
Dense clusters of yellow flowers in spring. Zones 3-9.
  'Herman's Pride': silvery markings on leaves; habit less invasive.
  'Variegatum' (ve-ri-e-GAH-tum): silver-variegated foliage.

Kniphofia uvaria

Lamium maculatum 'Aureum'

Lamium maculatum 'Beacon Silver'

Lamium maculatum 'White Nancy'

Lamium galeobdolon 'Herman's Pride'

Lathyrus latifolius

L. maculatum (ma-kew-LAH-tum)
Spotted Deadnettle
Variegated foliage. Clusters of pink to purple or white flowers in spring. Height 8-12" (20-30cm).

'Aureum' [subsp. *aureum*]: golden yellow leaves with creamy midribs. Habit less aggressive. Prefers at least some shade.

'Beacon Silver': compact form grows to 4-8" (10-20cm). Silver leaves with green edges; flowers pink.

'Chequers': silver-variegated foliage and amethyst-violet flowers. Height 9-12" (23-30cm).

'White Nancy': green-edged silver leaves often last through winter; flowers white. Height 6-8" (15-20cm). Spreads rapidly.

LATHYRUS (LATH-i-rus) ☼ ✂ ₩
Vetchling, Wild Pea
L. latifolius (la-ti-FOH-li-us)
Everlasting Pea, Perennial Sweet Pea
Vigorous flowering vine clings with tendrils or sprawls to 4-9' (1.3-2.7m). Best in rich, well-drained soils. Tolerates some shade. Showy rose-pink or white flowers open from summer to fall. Plant to grow on fence or trellis, or where plants can scramble over stones or rocks. Remove faded blossoms to extend season. Self-seeding, allow some seed-pods to ripen for spread and propagation. Naturalized.
Zones: 3-8, heat 8-1
Spacing: 30-40" (75-100cm)
Propagation: seed

Perennials that grow close to or in woodland often need sun and ample moisture early in the year but tolerate shade and drier soil in summer. Tree roots can deplete the soil of nutrients as well as moisture: adjust fertilization and watering as needed.

☼ = Full Sun		✂ = Cut Flowers	
☁ = Partial Sun/Shade		🌲 = Evergreen	
☁ = Shade		🦋 = attracts Butterflies	
₩ = Groundcover		🦅 = attracts Hummingbirds	

LAVANDULA (la-VAN-dew-la) ☀ 🌲 ✂ 🦋
L. angustifolia (an-goos-ti-FOH-li-a)
English Lavender
Bushy evergreen perennial with fragrant foliage and flowers. Best in moist, rich, yet well-drained soil. Useful in herb garden, border, or trimmed for low hedge. Semi-evergreen gray foliage topped by spikes of blue to purple flowers in summer. Flowers retain fragrance after drying. Mulch for winter protection in cold climates. Prune out older woody stems in spring to prevent overcrowding.
Zones: 5-9, heat 12-7
Spacing: 20-30" (50-75cm)
Propagation: division in early spring

LEONTOPODIUM (lee-on-to-POH-di-um)
L. alpinum (al-PY-num)   ☀ 〰
Edelweiss
Gray-leaved alpine for dry rocky places. Height 6-12" (15-30cm). Best in very well-drained, gritty alkaline soil. Useful for accent or mass planting, in rock garden or wall. Bright star-like flowers in summer are tiny yellow flower clusters surrounded by gray or white woolly bracts. Short-lived; intolerant of excess moisture.
Zones: 2-7
Spacing: 8-10" (20-25cm)
Propagation: division, seed

LEUCANTHEMUM (loo-KAN-the-mum)
L. Xsuperbum   ☀ ☁ ✂ 🦋
[*Chrysanthemum maximum*,
   Chrysanthemum Xsuperbum]
Shasta Daisy
Free-flowering summer daisies grow to height of 24-30" (60-75cm). Foliage deep green, coarsely toothed. Flowers white, single or double. Best in full sun and in especially well-drained locations. Space 18-24" (45-60cm) apart. Cut tops to ground after killing frost in fall; apply winter mulch in cold areas. Zones 4-10.

   'Aglaia' (double): grows to 28" (70cm); big flowers have fringed petals.
   'Alaska' (single): hardy in zone 3; pure white petals with yellow centers; flowers 3" (8cm) across on 24-36" (60-90cm) stems.
   'Becky' (single): big flowers rise 36" (90cm) high, summer through fall with regular deadheading. Dark green foliage, evergreen in the South. Performs well in warmer climates.
   'Little Princess' (single): large flowers; compact 12" (30cm) plant.
   'Thomas Killen' (single): very large flowers have double row of white petals around crested gold center; vigorous, robust growth to 30" (75cm).
Zones: 4-9, heat 12-1
Spacing: 12-24" (30-60cm)
Propagation: division, seed

In the Swiss mountains, edelweiss (*Leontopodium alpinum*) was frequently carried down from regions of perpetual snow as proof of the climbers' achievements. The plant's survival became threatened, and it remains a protected species in some districts.

Lavandula angustifolia

Leontopodium alpinum

Leucanthemum Xsuperbum 'Little Princess'

Leymus arenarius 'Glaucus'

Leymus (LAY-mus) ☀

[*Elymus* (EL-i-mus)]
Wild Rye, Lyme Grass
L. arenarius 'Glaucus' (a-re-NAH-ri-us GLAW-kus)
European Dune Grass, Lyme Grass
Vigorously spreading ornamental grass prevents soil erosion, especially on sandy, coastal dunes. Prefers well-drained soil. Height to 24" (60cm). Deep gray-blue foliage; color best in hot, dry climates. Tall gray-green to yellow flower clusters in late summer.
Zones: 4-9
Spacing: 18-24" (45-60cm)
Propagation: division in early spring

Liatris (lee-AH-tris) ☀ ☁ ✂ 🦋

Blazing-star, Gay-feather
Summer-blooming perennials on tuberous roots. Best in well-drained soil; plant 4-6" (10-15cm) deep. Accent for border, container, for cutting and drying. Flowers open from top of each stiffly erect spike. Naturalized.
Zones: 3-9, heat 9-2
Spacing: 18-24" (45-60cm)
Propagation: seed (species), division

L. pycnostachya (pik-noh-STAK-ee-a)
Kansas Gay-feather
Mauve or white flowers open on feathery spikes. Grass-like foliage forms clump at base and clothes flowering stems. Height 3-5' (0.9-1.5m). Heavy, 15-18" (38-45cm) long flower spikes may need support. Intolerant of excess winter moisture.

L. scariosa (ska-ri-OH-sa)
Tall Gay-feather
White or purple varieties with fewer leaves on flowering stems. Height 2-4' (0.6-1.2m). Hardy in zone 2.

L. spicata (spee-KAH-ta)
Spike Gay-feather
Mauve or white varieties, on attractive 6-15" (15-38cm) spikes. Leaves progressively smaller up the flower stems. Height 24-36" (60-90cm).

Liatris spicata

Liatris pycnostachya

LIGULARIA (lig-ew-LAH-ri-a) ☼ ☁ ✄

Bold accents for moist, cool places. Prefer well-drained yet constantly moist, rich soil. Large, often decorative leaves. Mid to late summer daisy-like flowers in loose clusters or tall spikes. Use baits to deter slugs and snails.
Zones: 4-8, heat 8-1
Spacing: 24-36" (60-90cm)
Propagation: division in spring, seed (species)

L. dentata (den-TAH-ta)
Bigleaf Ligularia, Bigleaf Golden-ray
Long-stemmed, toothed leaves to 20" (50cm) wide, useful for cut arrangements. Clusters of orange flowers.
   'Desdemona': bronze foliage with purple undersides.

L. przewalskii (sha-VAL-skee-y)
Shavalski's Ligularia
Deeply cut leaves, blackish stems, and tall narrow spikes of yellow blossoms. Height 4-6' (1.2-1.8m).

L. stenocephala (sten-oh-KEF-a-la)
Narrow-spiked Ligularia
Coarsely toothed leaves, purplish stems, with bright yellow flowers in spikes that rise 4-6' (1.2-1.8m).
   'The Rocket' (may be listed as *L. przewalskii* cv.): 18-24" (45-60cm) spikes of lemon-yellow flowers.

Ligularia dentata 'Desdemona'

Ligularia stenocephala 'The Rocket'

Ligularia przewalskii

Lilium lancifolium

Lilium Oriental Hybrids

LILIUM (LIL-i-um) ☀ ☁ ✂

Lily

Large-flowered bulb plants for border, patio, container, fresh cut flowers. Showy, colorful and sometimes fragrant flowers carried several to many per leafy stem. Flower forms include narrow to broad trumpets, bowl-shaped and flat blossoms, and the recurved petals of tiger lilies. For indoor decoration, remove stamens to avoid pollen stains. Lilies that have been brought into flower out-of-season may not flower in their first season outdoors. Grow in fertile, well-drained soil with plenty of water.

Zones: 3-9, heat 8-4
Spacing: 10-20" (25-50cm)
Propagation: bulb scales, offsets, bulbils, seed

Asiatic hybrids
Bloom in early summer, 2-4' (0.6-1.2m) tall. Many colors. Most have trumpet flowers that face up, down or outwards; some flat or recurved.

Oriental hybrids
Summer to early fall flowering, heights from 3' to 5' (0.9m to 1.5m). Big range of colors and flower forms.

L. lancifolium (lan-si-FOH-li-um, lan-ki-FOH-li-um) [*L. tigrinum* (ty-GREE-num)]
Tiger Lily
Showy, turk's-cap flowers in summer. Spreads vigorously from bulbils that develop in leaf axils. Good for naturalizing.

L. regale (re-GAH-lee)
Royal or Regal Lily, Easter Lily, Christmas Lily
Frequently grown in containers for early spring decoration, 3-5' (0.9-1.5m) tall. White blooms open naturally late spring to early summer.

LIMONIUM (li-MOH-nee-um) ☀ ✂

L. latifolium (la-ti-FOH-li-um)
Statice, Sea Lavender, Marsh Rosemary
Huge airy sprays of tiny, blue-violet flowers spread in mid to late summer above dense green leafy mound. Height 24-30" (60-75cm), spread 18-24" (45-60cm). Long-lasting flowers good for cutting and drying. Performs well in coastal conditions; best in moist, deep loamy soil.

Zones: 3-9, heat 12-3
Spacing: 24-30" (60-75cm)
Propagation: seed

Lilium regale

Limonium latifolium

LINUM (LY-num) ☀ ⛅
Flax

Reliable, clump-forming plants have feathery foliage and delicate yellow or blue flowers continuously from late spring or early summer. Best in light, well-drained soil. Useful in rock garden, at front of border, in natural planting. Tend to be short-lived but readily self-seed.
Zones: 5-8, heat 8-2
Spacing: 12-18" (30-45cm)
Propagation: seed, division

L. flavum (FLAH-vum)
Golden Flax

Big, loose clusters of 1" (2.5cm) yellow flowers in summer. Height 12-24" (30-60cm). Apply light winter mulch to protect near-woody stems.

L. narbonense (nar-boh-NEN-see)
Narbonne Flax

Slightly cup-shaped blue flowers in summer. Height 18-24" (45-60cm). Cut stems back to about 8" (20cm) after flowering, and apply mulch for winter protection in colder areas.

L. perenne (pe-REN-nee)
Perennial Flax

Upright, dainty stems bear azure-blue flowers that open continuously from late spring. Tolerates partial shade, where flowering period can last 12 weeks. Height 12-18" (30-45cm). Prune back after flowering to maintain attractive plant form. Hardy to zone 4.

LIRIOPE (li-RY-oh-pay) ☀ ⛅ ☁ 〰 🌲
Lilyturf

Spreading, mounding grass-like member of the lily family with clustered white or blue to purple flowers in summer. Thrives in any well-drained soil, sun or shade. Excellent as edging or low accent for border, or groundcover around trees and on slopes. Foliage may be damaged by ice and winds of northern winters.
Zones: zones 4 or 6-10; heat 8-3
Spacing: 12-15" (30-38cm)
Propagation: division

L. muscari (mus-KAH-ri)
Big Blue Lilyturf

Late summer flowers are white or shades of blue-purple. Dark berries persist into winter. Fleshy, strap-like leaves. Mounds 12-18" (30-45cm). Plant lighter color flower and variegated leaf varieties in partial shade. Hardy to zone 6.

L. spicata (spee-KAH-ta)
Creeping Lilyturf

Hardier species for zones 4-10. Summer flower spikes rise above mounded leaves to height of 8-12" (20-30cm). Pale lilac or whitish blossom, blue-black berries. Hardy to zone 4.

Install tree rings and suitable edgings between flower beds and lawn to make mowing easier and reduce the need for trimming. A 4-inch deep (10cm) edging will keep most grasses and spreading perennials within bounds. Steel, aluminum or vinyl strips, sunk into the ground, make an inconspicuous edging.

Linum flavum

Linum perenne

Liriope spicata

Lobelia cardinalis

LOBELIA (loh-BEE-li-a) ☼ ⛅ 🦋 🐦

Vigorous perennials with brilliant summer flowers in colors that range from deep scarlet to dark blue. Prefer rich, moist yet well-drained soil; tolerate wet conditions. Good for accents, natural plantings. Tall clusters of tubular or star-like flowers on stiff stems. Lift and divide clumps every 3 years to maintain vigor. Often short-lived though selfseeding can perpetuate display. Apply protective mulch or lift and protect for northern winters.
Zones: 2-9, heat 9-2
Spacing: 18-24" (45-60cm)
Propagation: division, seed

L. cardinalis (kar-di-NAH-lis)
Cardinal Flower
Showy cardinal-red blossoms on 24" (60cm) spikes rise to 2-4' (0.6-1.2m). Foliage dark green or red-bronze.

L. siphilitica (si-fi-LIT-i-ka)
Great Lobelia, Blue Cardinal Flower
Blue flowered spikes rise to 24-36" (60-90cm) in late summer. Leaves slightly downy. Grows well in moist, even boggy, soils. Zones 4-8.

LUNARIA (loo-NAH-ri-a) ⛅ ✂

L. annua (AN-ew-a)
[*L. biennis* (by-EN-is)]
Honesty, Silver-dollar Plant, Money Plant
Self-seeding biennial for partial shade. Thrives in any well-drained garden soil. Fragrant white to purple spring flowers followed by unusual, rounded, 2" (5cm) paperthin fruits, silvery when dry. Cut stems just as green color fades from fruit; hang to dry in cool airy place for 3-5 weeks.
Zones: 4-8, heat 8-1
Spacing: 15-20" (38-60cm)
Propagation: seed

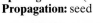

Lunaria annua

Lobelia siphilitica

LUPINUS (loo-PEEN-us) ☀ ⛅ ✂ 🦋 🐦

Lupine

Vigorous though short-lived perennials valued for colorful spring and summer flowers. Wild forms reseed in natural plantings. Good winter drainage essential.

Note: seeds and seedpods are poisonous.

Zones: 4-6, heat 9-1

Spacing: 24-30" (60-75cm)

Propagation: seed

L. 'Russell Hybrids'

Showy, colorful upright flowering spikes. Height 3-4' (0.9-1.2m). Good in mixed borders and for massed plantings. Prefer rich, moist yet well-drained, neutral to acid soil. Attractive mounds of grayish or bright green, palmately lobed leaves. Densely packed, long flower clusters in clear white or shades of blue, purple, red, pink, cream, and yellow. Best where summer nights are cool.

L. perennis (pe-REN-nis)

Wild Lupine

Deep-rooted wildflower with upright spikes of early summer blossoms rising to about 24" (60cm). Best in well-drained, acid, sandy soil; tolerates poor dry conditions. Good for natural planting, borders. Flowers are usually blue, sometimes pink or white.

LYCHNIS (LIK-nis) ☀ ✂ 🐦

Campion, Catchfly

Upright plants with bright summer flowers. Good drainage essential in cold areas. Useful in borders and natural landscapes where plants readily self-seed.

Zones: 3-9, heat 7-1

Spacing: 12-15" (30-38cm)

Propagation: seed, division

L. Xarkwrightii (ark-RYT-ee-y)

Arkwright's Campion

Brilliant orange-scarlet flowers are borne above dark bronze foliage. Grows 18-24" (45-60cm). Pinch early in the season to force additional shoots and reduce potential legginess.

L. chalcedonica (kal-se-DOH-ni-ka)

Maltese-cross

Rounded clusters of small, deep scarlet, Maltese-cross-shaped flowers rise 24-36" (60-90cm). Prefers consistent moisture. Dark green leaves contrast well with flower color. Naturalized.

L. coronaria (ko-roh-NAH-ree-a)

Rose Campion

Informal, loose clusters of purplish, pink, or white flowers rise to 30" (75cm). Leaves and stems felted with gray-white hairs.

Lupinus 'Russell Hybrids'

Lychnis X*arkwrightii*

Lychnis coronaria

Lychnis viscaria

Lysimachia clethroides

Lychnis chalcedonica

Lysimachia nummularia

L. viscaria (vis-KAH-ri-a)
German Catchfly
Magenta flower clusters top 12-18" (30-45cm) plants in early summer. Tolerates dry conditions. Leafy tufts at base. Stems tend to be sticky. Needs some shade in southern zones.

LYSIMACHIA (ly-si-MAH-ki-a) ☼ ☁
Loosestrife
Vigorously spreading perennials with either upright or prostrate stems. All prefer rich, moist, yet well-drained soils. Leaf margins smooth. Flowers rounded or bellshaped, borne singly or in narrow spikes.
Zones: 3-8. heat 9-3
Spacing: 24-24" (30-60cm)
Propagation: division, seed

L. clethroides (kleth-ROI-deez)
Gooseneck Loosestrife
Spreading clump has white late summer flowers on slender, arching spikes. Useful in natural planting; frequent division contains exuberant spread in formal border.

Height and spread 24-36" (60-90cm). Space 30-36" (75-90cm).

L. nummularia (nu-mew-LAH-ri-a) 〰 🌲
Creeping Jenny, Moneywort, Creeping Charlie
Rapidly spreading naturalized creeper mounds 4-8" (10-20cm) high. Grows well in moist or wet conditions. Good groundcover near streams and pools. Smoothly rounded leaves. Fragrant, bright yellow flowers open in early summer. Naturalized.
   'Aurea' (AW-ree-a): yellow leaves. Prefers partial shade.

L. punctata (punk-TAH-ta) ✂
Yellow Loosestrife
Lemon yellow blossoms open in early summer on stiffly erect flowering spikes. Height 12-24" (30-60cm). Tolerates either wet or dry soil. Best in partial shade. Naturalized.
   'Alexander' (PP 10598): foliage is tinted pink when young, maturing to green with gold variegations.

The sitcky stem-joints of German catchfly *(Lychnis viscaria)* are said to protect its flowers from infestation by ants and other insects.

Lythrum (LITH-rum) ☼ ☁ 🦋 ➤
Lythrum, Loosestrife
L. virgatum (vir-GAH-tum)
Purple Loosestrife
Upright, clump-forming perennials for moist locations. Useful in borders and well-defined natural plantings (see note below). Willow-like leaves. Small summer flowers are pink or purple, in showy spikes on long 4-angled stems. Named hybrids offer variety of color and height.
  'Morden Gleam': bright carmine flowers on spikes that rise to 36" (90cm).
  'Morden Pink': rose-pink flowers top 36-48" (90-120cm) plants.
Zones: 3-9, heat 9-1
Spacing: 15-18" (38-45cm)
Propagation: division

NOTE: Naturalized *Lythrum* species can rapidly become very invasive, especially in wetlands. All cultivation of lythrum is prohibited in a number of states: check with your State Department of Natural Resources for current restrictions.

Macleaya (mak-LAY-a) ☼
M. cordata (kor-DAH-ta)
Plume Poppy
Handsome large perennial grows 5-10' (1.5-3.0m) tall. Best in rich, well-drained soil. Useful accent specimen with attractive foliage and feathery summer flowers; or plant as background in border display. Broad, lobed gray-green leaves have silvery undersides. Creamy white plumes of blossom are 10-12" (25-30cm) long. Spreads vigorously.
Zones: 3-8, heat 12-7
Spacing: 5' (1.5m)
Propagation: division, root cuttings, seed

Before first frost, let water drain out of hosepipes. If the hose end is sealed by a spray nozzle, just one night of early or unexpected freeze can result in a burst faucet supply pipe. Once nights regularly fall below freezing, disconnect the hose from the faucet after each use. Store unused, empty hoses in the garage or shed.

Malva cordata

Lythrum virgatum

Malva moschata

Malva alcea

MALVA (MAL-va) ☀ ☁ 🦋
Mallow
Informal, free-flowering perennials naturalized in North America. Prefer dry, alkaline soil; in warmer areas, plant in deeper, richer soil. Useful in mixed borders and self-seeding in natural plantings. Flowers white or pink, summer and early fall. Short-lived plants easily grown from seed.
Zones: 4-8, heat 8-1
Spacing: 12-18" (30-45cm)
Propagation: seed, division

M. alcea (al-SEE-a)
Hollyhock Mallow
Loose clusters of rose to white flowers. Grows 24-36" (60-90cm) tall. Light green foliage.
   'Fastigiata' (fa-sti-gi-AH-ta): 2" (5cm) rose-pink flowers on upright, well-branched plant; height 3-4' (0.9-1.2m).

M. moschata (mos-KAH-ta)
Musk Mallow
Symmetrical, shrubby plants grow to 36" (90cm) tall. Dark green feathery foliage and rose or white flowers.

Apply a winter mulch to the less hardy perennials before the ground freezes. This will protect their crowns, which are usually above the soil surface, against freezing conditions. Then, after the ground first freezes hard in winter, apply a mulch to protect the hardier herbaceous perennials. Use fallen leaves (preferably not from city streets), grass clippings, sawdust, coarse peat moss, or other organic material for the mulch. This protective cover must be removed as new growth starts and the ground begins to warm up next spring, or there will be delays in early growth.

☀ = Full Sun   ✂ = Cut Flowers
☁ = Partial Sun/Shade 🌲 = Evergreen
☁ = Shade   🦋 = attracts Butterflies
〰 = Groundcover   🦅 = attracts Hummingbirds

MARRUBIUM (ma-ROO-bi-um) ☼
M. vulgare (vul-GAH-ree)
Horehound, Hoarhound
Vigorous, spreading herb grows 18-30" (45-75cm) high.
Velvety, downy foliage and stems used to flavor medi-
cines, tea, candy. Grows in any well-drained soil. Natu-
ralized member of the Mint family.
Zones: 4-9, heat 10-2
Spacing: 10" (25cm)
Propagation: seed, division

MELISSA (me-LIS-a) ☼ ☁
M. officinalis (o-fi-si-NAH-lis)
Lemon Balm
Rapidly spreading herb grows 24-36" (60-90cm) high.
Light, dry soils enhance flavor. Lemon-scented leaves
used in teas, soups, to season veal and poultry, and in
toiletries. Small white flowers cluster in leaf axils on
square stems. Naturalized member of the Mint family.
Zones: 4-10
Spacing: 18" (45cm)
Propagation: seed, division, cuttings

MENTHA (MEN-tha) ☼ ☁ 〰
Mint
Spreading herbs with square stems and small blue, pink,
or white flowers. Best in rich, moist, slightly acid soil.
May become invasive.
Zones: 4-10, heat 12-1
Spacing: 12-15" (30-38cm)
Propagation: division

M. Xpiperita (py-pe-REE-ta)
Peppermint
Height 12-24" (30-60cm). Reddish-green stems, fragrant leaves, and dense spikes of violet flowers in late
summer.

M. pulegium (poo-LEG-i-um)
Pennyroyal
Aromatic groundcover with creeping stems and spikes
of lavender-blue or pink summer flowers. Height 18-24"
(45-60cm). Bitter-tasting leaves and stems once used in
medicines, now as insect repellent. Hardy to zone 7.

Marrubium vulgare

Mentha Xpiperita

Melissa officinalis

Mentha spicata

m

Mentha suaveolens

Mertensia virginica

M. spicata (spee-KAH-ta)
Spearmint
Strongest mint, used to flavor teas, sauces, jellies, salads, vegetables, and in cooking meats. Height 12-24" (30-60cm). Dense spikes of violet or pink flowers rise above green foliage. Cut leafy stems freshen and perfume a room and repel flies. Naturalized.

M. suaveolens (swah-vee-OH-lenz)
[*M. rotundifolia* (roh-tun-di-FOH-li-a)]
Apple Mint, Pineapple Mint
Height 6-36" (15-90cm). Rounded, wrinkled, downy, 1-4" (2.5-10cm) leaves. Grayish white flower clusters become pink or violet. Cut leafy stems freshen and perfume a room and repel flies. Naturalized.

MERTENSIA (mer-TEN-zi-a)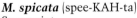
M. virginica (vir-JIN-i-ka)
Virginia Bluebells
Spring-blooming, summer dormant perennial has nodding clusters of blue, bell-shaped flowers. Height 12-24" (30-60cm). Prefers rich, acid, moist soil. Grow in shady border, woodland or natural garden. Gray-green oval leaves. Flower buds pink, turning blue as they open and mature. Naturalized.
Zones: 3-9, heat 7-1
Spacing: 12-16" (30-40cm)
Propagation: seed

Miscanthus sinensis var. purpurascens

MISCANTHUS (miz-KAN-thus) ☼ ⛅ ✂
Silver Grass

Large, upright, clump-forming ornamental grasses for accent, screen. Best in deep, fertile soil that has plenty of available moisture but is not soggy. Leaf blades have white midribs, rough margins. Flowers in feathery-looking flat or fan-shaped clusters (panicles). Cut top growth back in late winter.

Zones: 5-9, heat 8-1
Spacing: 2-5' (0.6-1.5m), depending on species
Propagation: division in spring

M. sinensis (sy-NEN-sis)
Japanese Silver Grass, Eulalia Grass
Dense clumps of cascading foliage grow to 7' (2.1m) high. Tolerates moisture; suitable for waterside planting. Fan-shaped flower clusters open red, become white with age, remain attractive through winter. Winter foliage almond or buff color. Clump centers die out with age. Most forms hardy in zone 4.

   '**Gracillimus**', Maiden Grass: slender dark green leaf blades; height to 5' (1.5m); leaf-tips curl in fall.
   '**Graziella**': white flower plumes rise well above slender foliage. Leafy clusters rise 4-5' (1.2-1.5m).

'**Morning Light**': green and white striped leaves; height to about 4' (1.2m).
'**Silberfeder**', Silverfeather Grass: medium green foliage and large silvery white plumes of flowers in summer.
'**Variegatus**' (ve-ri-e-GAH-tus), Variegated Silver Grass: graceful white-and-green striped leaves; height to 4' (1.2m); hardy in zones 5 and 6 only; needs partial shade.
'**Zebrinus**' (zee-BRY-nus), Zebra Grass: bright green foliage has yellow stripes across the blades; narrow, upright clump to 7' (2.1m); leaves have rusty-orange tips in winter.

M. sinensis var. *condensatus* (kon-den-SAY-tus)
Dense clump grows 5-6' (1.5-1.8m) high; broad, flat, white-ribbed leaves. Flower cluster opens burgundy, becoming bronze in winter.

M. sinensis var. *purpurascens* (pur-pew-RAS-enz)
Purpurascens Silver Grass
Smaller, upright variety grows 3-4' (0.9-1.2m) tall. Broad, dark green leaf blades. Flowers with silvery-white plumes in late summer. Plant turns brilliant red-orange in fall.

Miscanthus sinensis 'Gracillimus'

Miscanthus sinensis 'Graziella'

Miscanthus sinensis 'Silberfeder'

Miscanthus sinensis var. *purpurascens*

MOLINIA (moh-LIN-i-a) ☼ ⛅

M. caerulea (se-REW-lee-a)
Purple Moor Grass
Adaptable ornamental grass grows in tall, narrow tufts.
Height 5-8' (1.5-2.4m). Useful in borders and as accent.
Best in moist, well-drained, acid soil. Blue-gray leaves.
Purplish flower clusters (panicles) open in summer.
   'Variegata': yellow-striped green leaves.
Zones: 4-9, heat 9-5
Spacing: 15-24" (38-60cm)
Propagation: division

MONARDA (moh-NAH-da)

Wild Bergamot, Horsemint   ☼ ⛅ ✂ 🦋 🐦
Aromatic ornamental herbs with dense terminal clusters
of white, red, purplish or yellow flowers surrounded by
colorful bracts. Grows rapidly in rich, moist soil. Useful
spreaders for natural planting, accents in border. Mint
family. Sometimes used to mask odors in oils, perfumes.
Naturalized.
Zones: 4-9
Spacing: 12-15" (30-38cm)
Propagation: division

M. 'Marshall's Delight': pink flowers; height 2-3'
(60-90cm). Mildew resistant.

M. didyma (DID-i-ma)
Bee Balm
Summer flowers are red, pink, or white. Attract bees,
hummingbirds, and butterflies. Height 2-4' (0.6-1.2m).
   'Blue Stocking': violet blue flowers.
   'Cambridge Scarlet': very vigorous; flaming scarlet
   flowers.
   'Gardenview Scarlet': big, scarlet flowers; mildew
   resistant.
   'Jacob Cline': deep red flowers; mildew-resistant.
   'Petite Delight': Lavender rose; mildew resistant.

M. fistulosa (fis-tew-LOH-sa)
Wild Bergamot
Lavender flowers with whitish or purple bracts on 2-4'
(0.6-1.2m) plants. Hardy to zone 3.

Molinia caerulea 'Variegata'

Monarda didyma

Monarda didyma

Myosotis sylvatica

Nepeta cataria

Nepeta subsessilis

MYOSOTIS (my-o-SOH-tis)

Forget-me-not, Scorpion Grass

Short-lived, self-seeding perennials form clumps 6-18" (15-45cm) high. Best in moist, well-drained soils. Useful in rock gardens, on shaded banks, in woodland and natural plantings. Small clear blue spring to early summer flowers open in slightly coiled clusters resembling scorpion tails.

Zones: 3-8, heat 7-1
Spacing: 9-12" (23-30cm)
Propagation: seed, division

M. alpestris (al-PES-tris)
Alpine Forget-me-not
Small tufted plant grows to 6" (15cm). Naturalized.

M. scorpioides (skor-pi-OI-deez) ⋙
Water Forget-me-not
Naturalized species mounds 10-20" (25-50cm). Best in moist or boggy soils, beside stream, pond. Naturalized.

M. sylvatica (sil-VAT-i-ka)
Woodland Forget-me-not
Self-seeding annual or biennial species. Blue, pink or white flowers. Best with some shade. Soft, hairy leaves.

NEPETA (NEP-e-ta) ☼ ☁ ⋙ 🐱 🐦

Catmint

Spreading aromatic herb with gray-green leaves topped with spikes of clustering late spring flowers. Grows rapidly in rich, moist soils. Contain vigor with sandy, drier conditions. Useful as edging, in rock or herb gardens, natural plantings. Mint family.

Zones: 3-8, heat 12-2
Spacing: 12-18" (30-45cm)
Propagation: seed, division

N. cataria (ka-TAH-ri-a)
Catnip
Height 24-36" (60-90cm). Lemon-minty scent of crushed leaves delights cats. Used in teas. Flowers pale pink to white. Naturalized.

N. Xfaassenii (fah-SEN-ee-y)
[*N. mussinii* (mu-SEE-nee-y)]
Persian Ground Ivy, Persian Catmint
Bushy plants mounds 12-18" (30-45cm). Tolerates dry soil. Pale blue flowers from early summer. Trim off dead blooms to encourage second flowering. Useful edging plants. Several cultivars.
   'Blue Wonder': lavender-blue flowers; mounds to 15" (38cm).
   'Six Hills Giant': violet blue flowers rise 24-36" (60-90cm).

N. subsessilis (sub-seh-SIL-is)
Japanese Nepeta
Spreading herb with strong green leaves. Bluish purple flowers from summer to early fall. Prefers moist soils. Height to 24" (60cm).

Small perennial groups are easier to position for an attractive cluster when odd numbers of plants (3, 5, 7, or 9) are used rather than even numbers. Larger, massed plantings will absorb any number.

NIEREMBERGIA (nee-e-rem-BER-ji-a)
Cupflower
N. repens (REE-penz)
Whitecup, White Cupflower
Spreading tender perennial has delicate white, purple, or rose-tinted summer flowers. Forms mat 2-4" (5-10cm) high. Best in moist, well-drained soil. Useful edging and bedding plant, in rock gardens, between paving stones. Remove dead flowers and cut back in fall to encourage fresh spring growth. Mulch for winter protection. Grow as annual north of zone 7.
Zones: 7-9
Spacing: 6-12" (15-30cm)
Propagation: seed, division

During their first season, water perennials when the soil begins to dry. Early morning is the best time to water. Apply it at ground level, giving enough to soak around young roots to encourage them to grow more deeply into the prepared soil.

OENOTHERA (ee-no-THEE-ra)
Evening Primrose, Sundrops
Spreading, often shrubby perennials with showy paper-thin flowers in summer. Most are yellow, and many open in the evening. Thrive in well-drained, sandy soil. Naturalized.
Zones: see individual species for hardiness; heat 12-1
Spacing: 12-15" (30-45cm)
Propagation: division, seed, cuttings

O. fruticosa (froo-ti-KOH-sa)
Sundrops
Bright yellow blossoms open in terminal clusters on reddish, slender stems. Height 18-24" (45-60cm). Good border plant. Prefers dry soil. Zones 4-9.

O. macrocarpa (mak-roh-KAR-pa)
[*O. missouriensis* (mi-zoo-ri-EN-sis)]
Ozark Sundrops, Missouri Primrose
Spreading plant produces series of large, fragrant, 5" (13cm) bright yellow flowers. Each blossom lasts from evening to end of next day. Reddish growing tips turn upward. Height 6-12" (15-30cm). Useful groundcover for poor soils and full sun. Zones 3-8.

Nierembergia repens

Nierembergia repens

Oenothera macrocarpa

Oenothera speciosa

Origanum laevigatum 'Herrenhausen'

Oenothera tetragona

Origanum vulgare

O. speciosa (spee-si-OH-sa)
[*O. berlandieri* (ber-lan-dee-EH-ree)]
White or Showy Evening Primrose
Vigorous species for natural plantings, especially in warmer humid climates. Height 12-24" (30-60cm), spread 16-24" (40-60cm). Fragrant white flowers open during day, turn rose-pink with age. Plants often short-lived, self-seeding in good conditions. Zones 5-8.
　'Siskiyou': pale pink blossoms with white centers.

O. tetragona (tet-ra-GOH-na)
Four-angled Sundrops
Clusters of lemon yellow flowers open at night in late spring. Good border plant. Height 12-36" (30-60cm). Reddish-brown stems, well-branched plant, growing tips red. Short-lived perennial often treated as biennial. Zones 5-8.

ORIGANUM (o-RIG-a-num) ☀ 🦋
Marjoram, Oregano
Aromatic herbs good in containers, as edging, herb garden and border plants. Best in well-drained neutral to alkaline soils. Older stems become woody. Clusters of tiny flowers in summer. Leaves useful as culinary flavoring; plant parts also used medicinally.
Zones: see individual species for hardinesss; heat 10-2
Spacing: 8-15" (20-38cm)
Propagation: seed, division, cuttings

O. laevigatum 'Herrenhausen' (lee-vi-GAH-tum)
Ornamental Oregano
Upright growth to 15" (38cm). Dark foliage. Red-violet flowers all summer. Zones 4-9

O. vulgare (vul-GAH-ree)
Dittany, Marjoram, Oregano
Spreading, trailing mat grows 18" (45cm) tall. Tiny mauve flowers. Naturalized. Zones 3-10.

OSMUNDA (oz-MUN-da)
Flowering Fern
Hardy deciduous ferns for moist, shady locations such as sheltered borders, woodland. Most tolerate sun in moist conditions. Best in acid soil with plenty of organic matter; fertilize well. Naturalized.
Zones: hardiness 3-9, may vary by species; heat 9-1
Spacing: see individual species
Propagation: division, spores (sow as soon as ripe)

O. cinnamonea (sin-a-MOH-nee-a)
Cinnamon Fern, Fiddleheads, Buckhorn
Grows to 24-36" (60-90cm), taller in ideal conditions. Spreads slowly. New leaves pale green, becoming first darker green and then cinnamon brown for fall. Space 24-36" (60-90cm). Hardy to zone 2.

O. claytoniana (klay-to-nee-AH-na)
Interrupted Fern
Height 24-36" (60-90cm). Pale green foliage; outer sterile fronds larger than inner fertile ones. Space 36" (90cm). Hardy to zone 4.

O. regalis var. spectabilis (re-GAH-lis, spek-TAH-bi-lis)
Royal Fern, Flowering Fern
Slow spreading fern grows to 3-5' (0.9-1.2m), taller in wet conditions. Young fronds tinted brown or purple, turn dark green in summer and golden brown in fall. Space 3-4' (0.9-1.2m) apart. Hardy to zone 2.

PACHYSANDRA (pa-ki-SAN-dra)
P. terminalis (ter-mi-NAH-lis)
Japanese Spurge
Evergreen, stoloniferous groundcover for shaded areas. Height 9-12" (23-30cm). Prefers moist, well-drained soil; tolerates dry conditions. Plant in shade of trees, fence, building. Leaves dark glossy green, turn yellow in hot sun. Spikes of fragrant white flowers in late spring.
  'Green Carpet': compact, darker green form, 6-8" (15-20cm) high.
  'Silveredge': light green leaves have narrow silvery-white margins.
  'Variegata' (ve-ri-e-GAH-ta): white variegations; less vigorous form needs shade to prevent scorching.
Zones: 5-9, heat 8-3
Spacing: 12-20" (30-50cm)
Propagation: division, cuttings

Osmunda cinnamonea

Pachysandra terminalis 'Variegata'

Osmunda regalis var. *spectabilis*

Pachysandra terminalis

Paeonia lactiflora

Paeonia suffruticosa

Panicum virgatum
'Heavy Metal'

Panicum virgatum
'Shenandoah'

PAEONIA (pe-OH-ni-a)

Peony

Reliable, long-lived hardy herbaceous perennials or deciduous shrubs with huge showy blooms from late spring to early summer. Thrive in rich, well-drained soil. Fine in borders, as hedge, or accents in front of shrubs, wall, or fence. Compound leaves.
Zones: 3-8, heat 9-1
Spacing: 3-4' (0.9-1.2m)
Propagation: seed, division (herbaceous),
        cuttings (shrub)

P. lactiflora (lak-ti-FLOH-ra)
Chinese Peony, Common Garden Peony
Herbaceous, spreading clumps of erect and arching stems form mounds 2-4' (0.6-1.2m) high. Flowers single, semi-double, double, and anemone-form. Colors white and shades of pink, purple, red, sometimes yellow. New shoots red; protect against late freezes. Stake to support tall plants and large blooms. Plant with crown of red buds 1-2" (2.5-5cm) deep.

P. suffruticosa (suf-roo-ti-KOH-sa)
Tree Peony
Deciduous shrub grows 4-6' (1.2-1.8m) tall. Prefers partial shade. Tolerates moist soils. Useful in perennial or shrub border. Large flowers 6-10" (15-25cm) across, single or semi-double, in white and shades of pink, purple, and red. Characteristic fuzzy fruits. Slow growing. Flower colors fade in full sun. Space 5-8' (1.5-2.4m).

PANICUM (PAH-ni-kum)

P. virgatum (vir-GAH-tum)
Switch Grass
Perennial grass with decorative flowerheads to cut and dry. Leaves 18-24" (45-60cm) long on stiff, 4-7' (1.2-2.1m) stems. Flower clusters rise above upright leafy clumps, open pink, red or silvery, mature gray to brown. Fall color yellow, red or orange. Best in moist soil with full sun; shaded plants weaker, tend to collapse. Tolerates dry soil, coastal climates. Several cultivars. Naturalized.
 'Heavy Metal': upright clumps of blue-gray foliage 3-4' (0.9-1.2m) tall; with flowers, height reaches 4-5' (1.2-21.5m).
 'Shenandoah': bright red foliage from early summer. Clusters rise 3' (0.9m), 4' (1.2m) with flowers. Hardy only to zone 5.
Zones: 4-9, heat 9-1
Spacing: 10-15" (25-38cm)
Propagation: division, seed (species)

Paeonia suffruticosa

PAPAVER (pa-PAH-ver) ☼ ✄ ☖
Poppy
Showy, colorful, cup-shaped flowers rise singly on long flower stems above lobed or finely dissected foliage. Best in moist, well-drained soil. Must have good winter drainage. Characteristic milky sap.
Zones: hardiness 2-7, may vary by species; heat 9-2
Spacing: 8-18" (20-45 cm)
Propagation: seed, division in late summer

P. burseri (BUR-se-ry)
[P. alpinum (al-PY-num)]
Alpine Poppy
Self-seeding perennials for rock garden or edging use in zones 4-7. Height 8-10" (20-25cm). Semi-evergreen, gray-green, finely divided foliage. Silky, fragrant summer flowers in white, yellow, and pink. Short-lived perennial easily grown from seed. Intolerant of heat.

> If possible, use weathered rocks in rock gardens. Fresh-quarried limestone and sandstone may be so soft they break up within a few years.

P. nudicaule (new-di-KAW-lee) ☁ ∿
Iceland Poppy, Arctic Poppy
Tufting perennial with fragrant spring flowers, for rock garden, edging, front of border. Height 12-18" (30-45cm). Gray-green lobed foliage. Silky flowers yellow, greenish, orange, pink, red. Flowers first year from seed. Short-lived.

P. orientale (o-ree-en-TAH-lee)
Oriental Poppy
Flamboyant scarlet, orange, pink, white or bicolor early summer blooms have dark centers and purple-black marking at base of petals. Smooth, fringed or ruffled blooms. Height 18-36" (45-90cm). Good in mixed borders and natural plantings where other plants fill in when poppies become dormant. Strong green leaves die back in summer. Divide clumps every 3-6 years. Plant about 3" (8cm) deep, 20-30" (50-75cm) apart with crowns 3" (8cm) deep. New foliage often grows in fall. Mulch for winter protection.

Papaver orientale

Papaver nudicaule

Pennisetum alopecuroides 'Hameln'

Penstemon barbatus

Penstemon digitalis 'Husker Red'

p

PENNISETUM (pen-i-SEE-tum) ☀ ✂
Fountain Grass
P. alopecuroides (a-loh-pek-ew-ROI-deez)
Chinese Fountain Grass, Rose Fountain Grass
Compact ornamental grass forming dense, 24-36"
(60-90cm) mounds of graceful, arching bright green foli-
age. Useful border accent. Needs well-drained, fertile
soil. Flowers in summer; pinkish-white plumes mature
to rose-copper seedheads, good in dried arrangements.
  'Hameln': small form, growing to 18" (45cm).
Zones: 5-9, heat 9-2
Spacing: 24" (60cm)
Propagation: division, seed

PENSTEMON (pen-STEE-mon)
Beard-tongue   ☀ 🌤 🦋 🐦
Showy perennials best in moist, well-drained soil. Useful
for middle to back of borders, natural plantings, smaller
varieties for rock gardens. Nodding, tubular flowers in open
spikes. Colors range from white to pink, red, yellow and
blue. Easily grown from seed. Tolerate sunny, dry locations
though prolonged drought shortens plant life. Naturalized.
Zones: 3-8, heat 9-1
Spacing: 12-18" (30-45cm)
Propagation: seed, division, cuttings

P. barbatus (bar-BAH-tus)
Beardlip Penstemon, Common Beard-tongue
Semi-evergreen. Spring flowers pink or rose open from
the bottom of long spikes or racemes. Height 18-36"
(45-60cm). Hardy to zone 2.
  'Crystal': white flowers; grows 12-24" (30-60cm).
  'Pinifolius': orange-scarlet flowers, pine-like foliage;
   8" (20cm) tall.
  'Prairie Dawn': pale pink flowers.
  'Prairie Fire': deep red flowers; grows to 24" (60cm).

P. digitalis (di-ji-TAH-lis)
White Penstemon
Erect plant with purplish stems, grows 3-5' (0.9-1.5m) tall.
Early summer flowers are white or pink, in loose clusters.
  'Husker Red' (1996 Perennial Plant of the Year):
   red leaves and stems, with white flowers tinged pink;
   height 30-34" (75-85cm).

PEROVSKIA (pe-ROV-ski-a) ☼ ✂
P. atriplicifolia (a-tri-pli-si-FOH-li-a)
(1995 Perennial Plant of the Year)
Azure Sage, Russian Sage

Shrubby, aromatic, gray-green sage with pale blue summer flowers. Grows 3-5' (0.9-1.5m) tall. Prefers very well-drained soil. Useful border plant, in blue-gray groupings, with ornamental grasses, as low hedge or screen. Cut back to 12-18" (30-45cm) after first hard frost in fall or in spring. Loses upright form when grown with shade.

    'Filagrin': finely cut leaves; upright habit to 42" (100cm). Long flowering season.

    'Little Spire' (PPAF): short upright habit to 25" (63cm).

    'Longin': leaves broader than species; narrower, upright habit to 3-4' (60-120cm).

Zones: 5-9, heat 9-4
Spacing: 3-4' (0.9-1.2m)
Propagation: cuttings in summer, seed

PERSICARIA (per-si-KAH-ree-a) ☼ ⌇
Smartweed, Knotweed

Densely spreading, vigorous and often evergreen, clump-forming groundcovers. Grow well in moist soils. Numerous small flowers cluster in tight spikes. May become invasive.

Zones: 3-7, heat 8-1
Spacing: see individual species
Propagation: seed, division

P. affinis **'Border Jewel'** (a FEE-nis) 🌲
[*Polygonum affine* cv. (po-LIG-o-num)]
Compact leafy clumps grow to 4" (10cm) high. Useful groundcover for edging. Dark green foliage turns bright red in fall. Small spikes of light pink flowers. Space 9-12" (23-30cm).

P. bistorta **'Superbum'** (bis-TOR-ta soo-PER-bum)
[*Polygonum bistorta* cv.]
Clusters of big paddle-like lower leaves form mat rising to 24-36" (60-90cm). Good large area groundcover selection. Dense 6" (15cm) spikes of pink flowers in early summer; may bloom again in late summer.

Perovskia atriplicifolia

Persicaria affinis 'Border Jewel'

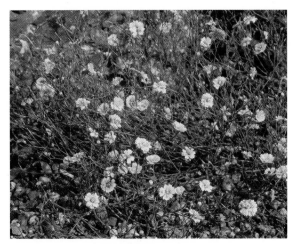

Petrorhagia saxifraga

Persicaria bistorta 'Superbum'

Phalaris arundinacea var. *picta*

PETRORHAGIA (pet-ro-RAH-gi-a) ☼ ⋎

P. saxifraga (sak-SIF-ra-ga)
[*Tunica saxifraga* (TEW-ni-ka)]
Tunic Flower, Coat Flower
Compact, spreader forms mat 4" (10cm) high. Best in poor, dry soils. Good edging, cover for rocky banks. Tufts of bristly, grass-like leaves; thin, wiry stems. White to pale purple summer flowers. Self-seeding.
Zones: 4-8
Spacing: 6-10" (15-25cm)
Propagation: seed

PHALARIS (fa-LAH-ris) ☼ ⛅ ⋎

Canary Grass
P. arundinacea var. ***picta*** (a-run-din-AY-see-a, PIK-ta)
Ribbon Grass, Gardener's-garters
Vigorous ornamental grass has bright green-and-white arching foliage. Height 24-36" (60-90cm). Useful in borders, as accent. Thrives in any fertile soil. Suitable for planting close to water. Narrow clusters of flowers open in summer. Leaf color fades in heat. Mow in late summer for fresh growth. May become invasive. Tolerates moist conditions, poorer soils and some shade with reduced vigor.
Zones: 3-9, heat 9-1
Spacing: 24" (60cm)
Propagation: division

☼ = Full Sun   ✂ = Cut Flowers
⛅ = Partial Sun/Shade 🌲 = Evergreen
☁ = Shade   🦋 = attracts Butterflies
⋎ = Groundcover   = attracts Hummingbirds

To dry flowers, tie in small bunches and hang upside down in an airy location. If this is not convenient, place in a container without water. After several weeks, flowers and stems will be dry.

Phlox paniculata

PHLOX (FLOKS) 🦋

Useful group of perennials provides bright flowers for most garden situations. Phlox grow best in well-drained soils. Stiff, sometimes woody, upright or prostrate stems bear lance-shaped or needle-like leaves. Clear flower colors range from white to pink to blue and purple, often with contrasting eyes. Naturalized.

Zones: 4-9, see species for variations; heat 9-4
Spacing: 12-18" (30-45cm); individual species may vary
Propagation: seed, cuttings, division

P. divaricata (dy-va-ri-KAH-ta) ☁☀ 〰
Wild Blue Phlox
Semi-evergreen spreader with open clusters of fragrant blue spring flowers. Height 12-15" (30-38cm). Good edging for shaded, moist yet well-drained sites.
> **'Fuller's White':** white flowers; height 8-12"(20-30cm); tolerates some sun.
> **var. *laphamii*** (lap-HAY-mee-y): dark blue flowers.

P. maculata (ma-kew-LAH-ta) ☀
Meadow Phlox, Wild Sweet William
Showy clusters of early summer flowers are mauve-pink, purple, or white. Height 24-36" (60-90cm). Good in border or natural planting. Thick, glossy dark green leaves, red-mottled stems. Earlier and better mildew resistance than border or garden phlox. Named cultivars.
> **'Miss Lingard'** [*P. carolina* cv.]: pure white flowers.

P. paniculata (pa-ni-kew-LAH-ta) ☀ ✂ 🐦
Border Phlox, Garden Phlox
Fragrant summer flowers are magenta, red, purple, pink, or white, in large dense pyramidal clusters. Height 3-4' (0.9-1.2m). Good for massed plantings or for accents in border. Needs some shade in hot dry climates. Tolerates moist soils. To help avoid powdery mildew infection, space 24" (60cm) or more for better air circulation. Cultivars often selected for mildew resistance. Hardy in zones 4-8.
> **'David' (2002 Perennial Plant of the Year):** highly fragrant white blossoms. Good mildew resistance.

P. stolonifera (stoh-lo-NIF-e-ra) ☁ 〰 🌲
Creeping Phlox
Low spreader forms dense cover 6-12" (15-30cm) high. Useful for shaded edging, rock garden. Very early spring flowers, violet to lavender. Very hardy; zones 2-8.
> **'Blue Ridge':** blue-lilac flowers.
> **'Bruce's White':** flowers white with yellow eye.

P. subulata (soo-bew-LAH-ta) ☀ 〰 🌲
Moss Phlox, Moss Pink
Spreading mounds covered with flowers in early spring. Height 6-9" (15-23cm). Best in sunny, well-drained sandy soil. Good edging, container, rock garden plant. Stiff, needle-like foliage on woody stems. Very hardy; zones 2-9.
> **'Candy Stripes':** bright two-tone white and pink flowers.

Phlox divaricata

Phlox maculata

Phlox paniculata

Phlox paniculata 'Darwin's Joyce'

Phlox stolonifera

Phlox subulata 'Candy Stripes'

PHYSALIS (FY-sa-lis) ☀ ☁ ✄
Ground Cherry, Husk Tomato
P. alkekengi (al-ke-KEN-gi)
[*P. franchetii* (fran-KET-ee-y)]
Chinese-lantern
Spreading perennial has ornamental orange seed-pods. Height 18-24" (45-60cm). Grows in any garden soil. Best in informal grouping. Oval foliage tends to hide small creamy-white summer flowers. Red fruits are encased in bright orange lantern-like calyces that lose color when left on plants. For drying, cut stems as leaves begin to die back; hang to dry in cool airy place for 3-5 weeks. Can be grown as an annual.
Zones: 3-9
Spacing: 24" (60cm)
Propagation: seed, division in spring

Woodland gardens look great in loose groups and as single plants, with open spaces between plantings and trees for mulch or leaf litter.

PHYSOSTEGIA (fy-so-STEE-ji-a)
P. virginiana (vir-ji-nee-AH-na) ☀ ☁ ✄ 🦋 🐦
Obedient Plant, False Dragonhead
Slender, upright perennial topped with spikes of pink to purple late summer flowers. Height 3-4' (0.9-1.2m). Prefers moist, acid, well-drained soil and full sun; tolerates drier soil with some shade. Good in border, natural planting. Heavy flowering stems need support. Divide clumps every 2-3 years. Spreads vigorously; may become invasive.
'Nana' (NAH-na): dwarf form grows to 12-18" (30-45cm).
'Summer Snow': flowers white; spreads less aggressively.
'Vivid': vibrant pink flowers; height 24-36" (60-90cm).
Zones: 2-9, heat 8-4
Spacing: 34-36" (60-90cm)
Propagation: seed, division

Physostegia virginiana

Physalis alkekengi

Physostegia virginiana 'Summer Snow'

Platycodon grandiflorus var. *mariesii*

Platycodon grandiflorus

Polemonium caeruleum

PLATYCODON (pla-ti-KOH-don) ☼

P. grandiflorus (gran-di-FLOH-rus)
Balloon Flower, Chinese Bellflower
Reliable perennial emerges late in spring and blooms all summer. Height 30-36" (75-90cm). Best in moist, well-drained soil. Provides good summer color in border or as accent. Oval, serrated leaves. Bell-shaped flowers open from inflated balloon-like buds. Blue-purple varieties best in full sun; pinks and whites tolerate some shade. Clumps do not spread and can remain undisturbed.

> ***P. grandiflorus* var. *mariesii*** (ma-REE-zee-y): compact form; height 12-24" (30-60cm); useful for edging or rock garden.
>
> **'Sentimental Blue'**: dwarf form grows to 6-8" (15-20cm).

Zones: 3-8, heat 9-3
Spacing: 12-24" (30-45cm)
Propagation: seed, division in spring

POLEMONIUM (po-le-MOH-ni-um) ⛅☼

Clump-forming perennials with informal, branching clusters of white, blue or purple flowers. Best in well-drained soil. Prefer cooler climates. Useful in partly shaded borders, at edge of woodland. Delicate, apple green fern-like leaflets.
Zones: 2-7, heat 8-1
Spacing: 18" (45cm)
Propagation: seed, division in fall

P. caeruleum (se-REW-lee-um) ✂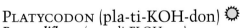
Jacob's-ladder, Greek Valerian, Charity
Summer flowers light to deep blue with yellow stamens. Height 18-24" (45-60cm).

P. reptans (REP-tanz)
Creeping Jacob's-ladder
Spring flowers in shades of pale blue. Height to 12" (30cm). Space 8-12" (20-30cm).

POLYGONATUM (po-li-go-NAH-tum)
Solomon's-seal

Rhizomatous plants with long, gracefully curving stems. Grow well in shady, moist, acid soil. Useful for damp woodlands, among shrubs, bulbs, in shaded borders and natural plantings. Handsome foliage for cut arrangements. Whitish bell-shaped late spring flowers hang below leaf nodes. Shining dark berries in fall.
Zones: 3-9, heat 9-1
Spacing: 16-24" (40-60cm)
Propagation: seed, division

P. biflorum (by-FLOH-rum)
Small Solomon's-seal
Height 24-36" (60-90cm). Leaves 4" (10cm) long on arching stems. Yellowish-white flowers. Naturalized.

P. commutatum (ko-mew-TAH-tum)
Great Solomon's-seal
Species for large-scale informal plantings. Height 3-7' (0.9-2.1m). Flowers yellow-green or whitish-green. Space 36-48" (90-120cm). Naturalized.

P. odoratum (oh-do-RAH-tum)
Solomon's-seal
Sweetly fragrant flowers are white with greenish markings. Height 18-24" (45-60cm).

POLYGONUM (po-LIG-o-num)
Fleece Flower
P. aubertii (aw-BER-tee-y)
Silver Fleece Vine, Silver-lace Vine, Russian Vine
Twining, deciduous woody vine can grow 10-15' (3.0-4.5m) in one season. Forms dense cover on fence or rocky bank. Profuse clusters of scented, fluffy white midsummer flowers. Growth fills available space.
Zones: 4-8, heat 8-1
Spacing: 4-8' (1.2-2.4m)
Propagation: seed, cuttings, division

P. affinis 'Border Jewel',
see *Persicaria* page 132
P. bistorta 'Superbum',
see *Persicaria* page 132
P. cuspidatum, P. japonicum, P. reynoutria,
see *Fallopia* page 85

Polygonum aubertii

Polygonatum commutatum

Polystichum acrostichoides

Potentilla atrosanguinea 'Gibson Scarlet'

Potentilla nepalensis 'Miss Willmott'

POLYSTICHUM (po-LIS-ti-kum)
P. acrostichoides (a-kro-sti-KOI-deez)
Christmas Fern

Evergreen fern has leathery, 24-36" (60-90cm) fronds that mature dark green. Spreads 10-14" (25-35cm) across. Useful in shaded border, light or deep woodland. Best in well-drained soil plenty of moisture. Naturalized.
Zones: 3-9, heat 9-1
Spacing: 12" (30cm)
Propagation: division, spores (sow as soon as ripe)

POTENTILLA (poh-ten-TIL-a)
Cinquefoil, Five-finger

Mounding, clumping, often herbaceous perennials with loose clusters of rose-like flowers in spring or summer. Best in light, sandy soil and where nights are cool. Useful in borders, some as groundcover and in rock gardens. Stems erect or sprawling.
Zones: 5-8, heat 9-4
Spacing: 12-20" (30-50cm)
Propagation: division, seed

P. atrosanguinea (at-roh-san-GWIN-ee-a)
Himalayan Cinquefoil

Summer-flowering potentilla mounds 18-30" (45-70cm). Prefers full sun. Trifoliate leaves are silky-hairy. Deep red flowers.

    'Gibson Scarlet': blood-red flowers and soft green foliage; grows to 18" (45cm).

P. nepalensis (ne-pa-LEN-sis)
Nepal Cinquefoil

Vigorous growth to 12-24" (30-60cm). Rosy-purple summer flowers. Leaves up to 12" (30cm) long. To maintain form, trim back severely after flowering.

    'Miss Willmott' ['Willmottae' (wil-MOT-ee)]: compact form 10-12" (25-30cm) high; carmine flowers have cherry-red centers.

P. neumanniana (noo-man-i-AH-na)
[*P. tabernaemontani* (ta-ber-nee-mon-TAH-ni),
  P. verna (VER-na)]
Spring Cinquefoil

Spreading, rooting stems form mat 6-9" (15-23cm) high. Spring flowers yellow. Rhizomatous.

    'Nana' [var. *nana* (NAH-na)]: dwarf form grows 3-4" (8-10cm) high. Golden-yellow flowers.

Potentilla neumanniana 'Nana'

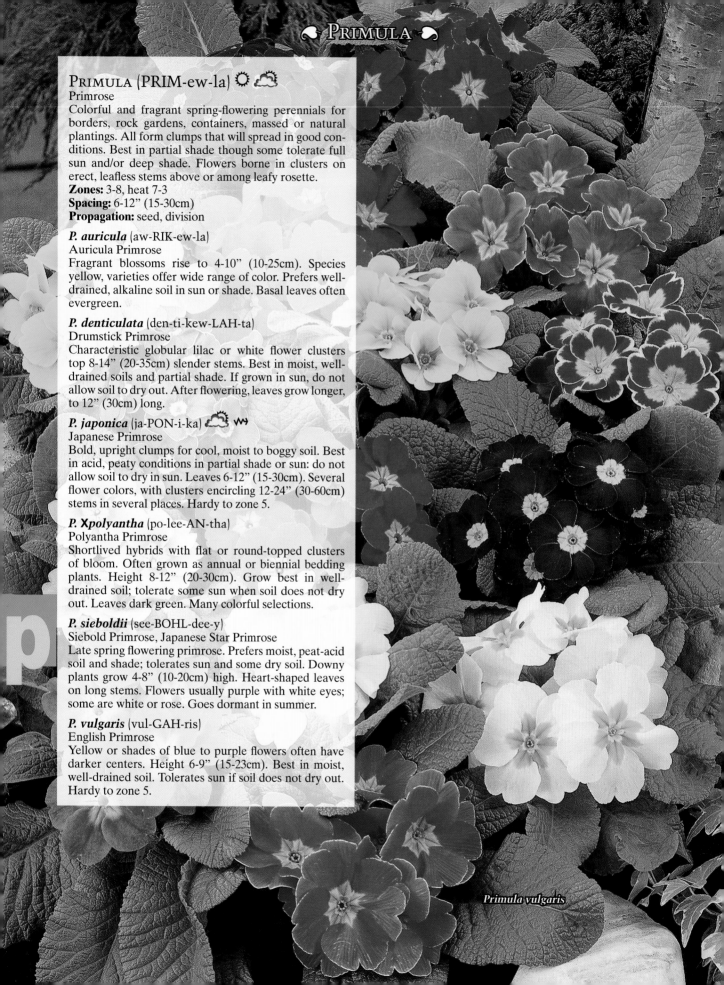

PRIMULA (PRIM-ew-la) ☀ ☁
Primrose

Colorful and fragrant spring-flowering perennials for borders, rock gardens, containers, massed or natural plantings. All form clumps that will spread in good conditions. Best in partial shade though some tolerate full sun and/or deep shade. Flowers borne in clusters on erect, leafless stems above or among leafy rosette.
Zones: 3-8, heat 7-3
Spacing: 6-12" (15-30cm)
Propagation: seed, division

P. auricula (aw-RIK-ew-la)
Auricula Primrose

Fragrant blossoms rise to 4-10" (10-25cm). Species yellow, varieties offer wide range of color. Prefers well-drained, alkaline soil in sun or shade. Basal leaves often evergreen.

P. denticulata (den-ti-kew-LAH-ta)
Drumstick Primrose

Characteristic globular lilac or white flower clusters top 8-14" (20-35cm) slender stems. Best in moist, well-drained soils and partial shade. If grown in sun, do not allow soil to dry out. After flowering, leaves grow longer, to 12" (30cm) long.

P. japonica (ja-PON-i-ka) ☁ 〰
Japanese Primrose

Bold, upright clumps for cool, moist to boggy soil. Best in acid, peaty conditions in partial shade or sun: do not allow soil to dry in sun. Leaves 6-12" (15-30cm). Several flower colors, with clusters encircling 12-24" (30-60cm) stems in several places. Hardy to zone 5.

P. Xpolyantha (po-lee-AN-tha)
Polyantha Primrose

Shortlived hybrids with flat or round-topped clusters of bloom. Often grown as annual or biennial bedding plants. Height 8-12" (20-30cm). Grow best in well-drained soil; tolerate some sun when soil does not dry out. Leaves dark green. Many colorful selections.

P. sieboldii (see-BOHL-dee-y)
Siebold Primrose, Japanese Star Primrose

Late spring flowering primrose. Prefers moist, peat-acid soil and shade; tolerates sun and some dry soil. Downy plants grow 4-8" (10-20cm) high. Heart-shaped leaves on long stems. Flowers usually purple with white eyes; some are white or rose. Goes dormant in summer.

P. vulgaris (vul-GAH-ris)
English Primrose

Yellow or shades of blue to purple flowers often have darker centers. Height 6-9" (15-23cm). Best in moist, well-drained soil. Tolerates sun if soil does not dry out. Hardy to zone 5.

p

Primula vulgaris

Primula denticulata

Primula japonica

Primula X*polyantha*

Primula vulgaris

PULMONARIA (pul-mon-AH-ri-a)

Lungwort

Low, spreading perennials. Use for edging, at front of shaded border, among bulbs. Spring flowers open with or before new foliage. Best in moist, well-drained soil. Lance-shaped leaves, sometimes speckled gray or silver.
Zones: hardiness 3-8, may vary by species; heat 8-4
Spacing: 10-12" (25-30cm)
Propagation: seed, division

P. angustifolia (an-goos-ti-FOH-li-a)

Blue Lungwort

Loose clusters of blue tubular flowers open from pink buds. Height 9-12" (23-30cm). Foliage green. Zones 2-7.

P. longifolia (lon-ji-FOH-li-a)

Long-leafed Lungwort, Joseph and Mary, Spotted Dog
Tight clusters of violet-blue flowers and white spotted, dark green leaves. Height to 12" (30cm); spread 18-24" (45-60cm).

'Bertram Anderson': deep blue flowers from pink tinted buds.

P. saccharata (sa-ka-RAH-ta)

Bethlehem Sage

Buds pink, mature flowers blue. Height 9-18" (23-45cm). Gray-speckled leaves persist long into fall, are sometimes evergreen.

'British Sterling': intensely silvery-white speckled leaves have contrasting green edges; height 12" (30cm).
'Margery Fish': more vigorous than species.
'Mrs. Moon': big, silver-spotted leaves.
'Pierre's Pure Pink': flowers open pink and stay pink.
'Sissinghurst White': flowers white; silvery marking on leaves.

PULSATILLA (pul-sa-TIL-a)

P. vulgaris (vul-GAH-ris)

[*Anemone pulsatilla* (a-NEM-oh-nee)]
European Pasqueflower

Spring flowering perennial for edging or rock garden. Big 2" (5cm), bell-shaped blue to reddish-purple flowers top 8-12" (20-30cm) stems. Characteristic fuzzy fruits persist after flowering. Foliage develops after flowers; finely divided, fern-like leaves mound 8-10" (20-25cm). Leave established plants undisturbed if possible.
Zones: 4-8, heat 7-5
Spacing: 10-12" (25-30cm)
Propagation: division, seed, root cuttings

Pulmonaria saccharata 'Sissinghurst White'

Summer color

Pulmonaria saccharata 'British Sterling'

Ranunculus repens

Pulsatilla vulgaris

Pulsatilla vulgaris

Rodgersia aesculifolia

RANUNCULUS (ra-NUN-kew-lus)

Buttercup, Crowfoot
R. repens (REE-penz)
Butter Daisy, Creeping Buttercup
Vigorous spreader has bright yellow summer flowers. Prefers moist soil. Use for informal groundcover. Naturalized species may become invasive. Leaves mound 6-12" (15-30cm). Flowering stems 18-24" (45-60cm) tall.

> **'Pleniflorus'** (plee-ni-FLOH-rus) ['Flore Pleno']: less vigorous, less invasive. Double yellow flowers rise to 18" (45cm).

Zones: 3-8, heat 8-2
Spacing: 15-18" (38-45cm)
Propagation: division, seed

RODGERSIA (rod-JER-si-a)

R. aesculifolia (es-kew-li-FOH-li-a)
Fingerleaf Rodgersia
Rhizomatous perennial with bold compound leaves. Late spring spires of white or pinkish blossom. Height 3-6' (0.9-1.8m). Leaves often bronze-green, stems clothed with brown hairs. Flower clusters 18-24" (45-60cm) long. Prefers moist, boggy soil. Tolerates full sun only where soil can remain constantly moist.

Zones: 5-7, heat 8-1
Spacing: 4-5' (1.2-1.5m)
Propagation: division in spring

ROSMARINUS (rohz-ma-REE-nus)
R. officinalis (o-fi-si-NAH-lis)
Rosemary
Tender, shrubby evergreen herb, height 24-36"
(60-90cm). Best in well-drained, slightly acid or neutral
soil. Gray-green, aromatic, needle-like leaves have many
culinary uses. Late winter or early spring flowers are
violet-blue, sometimes white. Trim in spring and after
flowering to encourage fresh leafy growth.
Zones: 7-10, heat 12-2
Spacing: 24-36" (60-90cm)
Propagation: cuttings

RUDBECKIA (rud-BEK-i-a)
Coneflower
Tall, showy, long-lasting blossoms from midsummer to
fall. Rapid growth in fertile, loose soil. Easy to grow in
borders, natural plantings. Daisy flowers have yellow to
orange petals, dark, high centers. Naturalized.
Zones: 3-10, heat 9-2
Spacing: 12-20" (30-50cm)
Propagation: seed, division in spring

R. fulgida (FUL-ji-da)
Black-eyed Susan, Orange or Showy Coneflower
Summer flowering plant grows 18-30" (45-75cm).
> **'Goldsturm' (1999 Perennial Plant of the Year):**
> compact and free-flowering; grows to 24" (60cm),
> big dark yellow flowers.
> **'Goldquelle':** lemon-yellow double flowers.

R. hirta (HER-ta)
Black-eyed Susan
Short-lived perennial often grown as annual or biennial.
Height to 36" (90cm). Deep yellow 2-3" (5-8cm) flowers.

Rosmarinus officinalis

Rudbeckia fulgida

Rudbeckia hirta

Ruta graveolens

Saccharum ravennae

Ruta (ROO-ta) ☼ ⛅ 🌲

R. graveolens (gra-VEE-oh-lenz)
Rue, Herb-of-grace
Shrubby herb grows 12-36" (30-90cm). Lacy, aromatic, blue-green foliage. Best in moist, light, well-drained soil. Useful foliage plant in border, herb garden, or as low hedge in milder climates. Summer flower clusters pale yellow. Trim back to old wood in spring to encourage fresh bushy growth.
Note: leaves may cause dermatitis.
Zones: 4-9
Spacing: 24" (60cm)
Propagation: seed, cuttings, division

Saccharum (sa-KAH-rum) ☼ ✂

S. ravennae (ra-VEN-ee)
[*Erianthus ravennae* (e-ri-AN-thus)]
Ravenna Grass, Plume Grass
Strong, vigorous, and hardy giant grass that grows 10-14' (3.0-4.2m) tall. Best in fertile, well-drained soil. Useful accent or screen. Smooth, stiff stems with 3' (0.9m) leaves become chestnut-brown in fall. Densely branched, silvery flower plumes open in late summer, turning beige as they mature and with cooler nights.
Zones: 5-9
Spacing: 2-5' (0.6-1.5m)
Propagation: division, seed

Sagina (sa-GEE-na) ☼ ⛅ ⛅ 〰 🌲

S. subulata (soo-bew-LAH-ta)
Corsican Pearlwort
Moss-like evergreen perennial with small leaves forming dense mats of foliage. Suitable for shady locations. Starry white flowers open on short stalks in midsummer. Height 2-4" (5-10cm).
Zones: 5-8
Spacing: 8-10" (20-25cm)
Propagation: division

Sagina subulata

SALVIA (SAL-vi-a) ☼ 🦋 🦅

Sage, Ramona

Reliable border plants with blue or gray-green leaves and summer or fall flowers from lavender to purple. Best in average to dry, acid, well-drained soil. Useful in borders, natural plantings, smaller varieties for rock gardens. Foliage and flowers often aromatic.

Zones: see individual species for hardiness; heat 12-1
Spacing: see individual species
Propagation: seed, division, cuttings

S. azurea (a-ZEW-ree-a)
Blue Sage, Azure Sage
Fall-flowering, grows 3-4' (0.9-1.2m). Dark green leaves larger at stem base. Azure-blue flowers borne in axils of smaller upper leaves, forming loose spikes. Space 30-40" (75-100cm). Zones 5-9. Naturalized.

  S. azurea* var. *grandiflora [*S. pitcheri* (PICH-er-y)]: paler green, bigger leaves, lighter colored flowers.

S. nemorosa (ne-mo-ROH-sa)
[*S.* X*superba* (soo-PER-ba), *S.* X*sylvestris* (sil-VES-tris)]
Violet Sage, Hybrid Sage
Dense spikes of violet-blue summer flowers rise 18-48" (45-120cm). Taller varieties need support. Tolerate heat and drought. Space 24-30" (60-75cm). Zones 4-7.

  'Blue Hill' ['Blauhügel', 'Bluemound']: pure blue flowers open over long period; compact habit, 16-20" (40-50cm) tall.

  'Blue Queen': rich violet flowers, height 18-24" (45-60cm).

  'East Friesland' ['Ostfriesland']: deep purple flowers, compact plants grow without support to 18" (45cm).

  'Lubeca': violet blue flowers for long season; grows 18-30" (45-75cm) tall.

  'May Night' (1997 Perennial Plant of the Year): larger, deep indigo blue flowers; height to 18" (45cm).

S. officinalis (o-fi-si-NAH-lis)
Common Sage, Garden Sage
Shrubby, semi-evergreen culinary herb has fuzzy 2" (5cm) gray-green leaves. Mounds 12-20" (30-50cm). Some forms have variegated foliage. Flowers small; purple, blue, or white. Space 12-16" (30-40cm). Zones 4-9.

S. pratensis (pra-TEN-sis)
[*S. haematodes* (hee-ma-TOH-deez)]
Meadow Clary, Meadow Sage
Bright lavender blue flower spikes top 12-36" (30-90cm) plants in summer. Long-stemmed basal leaves; few small leaves on flowering stems. Remove spent flowers to encourage later blooming. Tuberous species grows best in evenly moist soil. Space 24-30" (60-75cm). Zones 3-7.

S. verticillata 'Purple Rain' (ver-ti-si-LAH-ta)
Purple Rain Lilac Sage
Dark purple flowers on long spikes rise above 24" (60cm) mounds of broad, hairy leaves. Flowers from late spring through summer to early fall. Tolerates dry climates; attracts hummingbirds. Space 24" (60cm). Zones 5-7.

S

Salvia verticillata 'Purple Rain'

Salvia azurea

Salvia nemorosa 'Blue Hill'

Salvia nemorosa 'May Night'

Salvia officinalis 'Tricolor'

S

SANGUINARIA (san-gwi-NAH-ri-a)
S. canadensis (ka-na-DEN-sis)   ☀ ☁ ⋀⋀
Bloodroot
Woodland plant with white early spring blossoms and scalloped, roundish leaves. Grows 4-8" (10-20cm) high. Best in moist yet well-drained, acid, humus-rich soil in partial shade. Use in woodland, natural planting. Sap, stems, and rhizomes red. Naturalized.
Note: sap contains bitter alkaloid that can affect muscles and nerves if swallowed or absorbed through cut or scratch.
Zones: 3-8
Spacing: 8-12" (20-30cm)
Propagation: seed, division

SANGUISORBA (san-gwi-SOR-ba) ☀ ☁
Burnet
S. canadensis (ka-na-DEN-sis)
Canadian Burnet, Great Burnet, American Burnet
Large clump-forming perennial for moist locations. From summer to fall, white bottlebrush-like flowers rise 4-5' (1.2-1.5m) high. Grows vigorously in cool, damp soil. Useful in border, beside stream or pond, in boggy natural area. Compound leaves have sharply toothed leaflets. Naturalized.
Zones: 3-8
Spacing: 30-40" (75-100cm)
Propagation: seed, division

SANTOLINA (san-toh-LEE-na) ☀ ⋀⋀ 🌲
Compact, shrubby plants with aromatic finely-divided foliage. Grow best in well-drained soil; tolerate heat. Useful edging, low hedge, groundcover, or rock garden plants. Small, yellow, button-like flower heads in summer. Trim after flowering to maintain shape; prune older plants hard in spring.
Zones: 6-8, heat 12-1
Spacing: 18-24" (45-60cm)
Propagation: cuttings (summer)

S. chamaecyparissus (ka-mee-si-pa-RIS-us)
[*S. incana* (in-KAH-na)]
Lavender Cotton
Gray-green foliage mounds 12-24" (30-60cm). Useful groundcover plant for poor, stony soils. Prefers dry heat. Prune after flowering to shape new growth.

S. virens (VY-renz)
[*S. rosmarinifolia* (rohz-ma-ree-ni-FOH-li-a)]
Green Lavender Cotton, Holy Flax
Spreading sub-shrub has dark green, smooth foliage. Height and spread to 24 by 36" (60 by 90cm). Makes good low hedge.

A late frost can result in the loss of developing flower buds on peonies (*Paeonia* species) if the morning sun warms plants rapidly. One way to counteract this possibility is to cover plants with wet newspapers to slow down the thawing process. Another is to plant peonies in positions that are sheltered from the morning sun.

Sanguinaria canadensis

Sanguisorba canadensis

Santolina chamaecyparissus

Santolina virens

Saponaria ocymoides

Saponaria X lempergii 'Max Frei'

SAPONARIA (sa-poh-NAH-ri-a) ☼ 🦋 🐦
Soapwort
Easy to grow, vigorous perennials for banks, edging, walls, and rock gardens. Showy clusters of flowers open in summer. Trim back hard after flowering to encourage compact new growth.
Zones: 2-7, heat 8-1
Spacing: 9-12" (23-30cm)
Propagation: seed, division, cuttings

S. ocymoides (oh-ki-MOI-deez) 〰
Rock Soapwort
Trailing, mat-forming groundcover for dry, stony places. Height 4-9" (10-23cm). Flat, semi-evergreen leaves. Bright pink blossom.

> Remove winter mulch carefully to avoid damaging tender young shoots. If a late frost threatens, cover plants with newspapers or another temporary protective cover. Apply early fertilizer to the soil around the plant, avoiding contact with tender new growth.

S. officinalis (o-fi-si-NAH-lis)
Bouncing Bet
Clusters of pale pink flowers on upright stems that grow 12-24" (30-60cm) tall. Spreads to 18" (45cm). Naturalized. Zones 2-8.
   'Rosea Plena': clear pink flowers on neater, less vigorous plants

S. X lempergii **'Max Frei'** (lem-PUR-jee-eye) 〰
Large clusters of 1" (2.5cm) pink blossoms open from midsummer. Height 12-15" (30-38cm). Good edging, rock garden plant. Zones 3-7.

☼ = Full Sun	✂ = Cut Flowers
☁☼ = Partial Sun/Shade	🌲 = Evergreen
☁ = Shade	🦋 = attracts Butterflies
〰 = Groundcover	🐦 = attracts Hummingbirds

SATUREJA (sa-tew-REE-ya) ☼
Savory, Calamint
S. montana (mon-TAH-na)
Winter Savory
Low-growing, aromatic, mint family herb does well in any well-drained soil. Grows rapidly to 12-18" (30-45cm) high. Smooth, shiny leaves. Tender young leaves and stem tips flavor foods. Summer flowers white, pink, or purplish.
Zones: 5-8, heat 12-1
Spacing: 8-12" (20-30cm)
Propagation: seed, division, cuttings

Scabiosa columbaria 'Butterfly Blue'

Satureja montana

Scabiosa columbaria 'Pink Mist'

Scabiosa caucasica

SCABIOSA (skay-bee-OH-sa) ☼ ☁ ✂ 🦋
Pincushion Flower, Scabious
Colorful flowers like small pincushions attract butter-flies. Lower leaves provide dense foil for flowers. Plant groups in border for best display. Grow in moist, well-drained, neutral to alkaline soil. Prefers temperate climate. Best with partial shade in warmer areas.
Zones: 3-7; heat 8-3
Spacing: 12-15" (30-38cm)
Propagation: seed, division

S. caucasica (kaw-KAS-i-ka)
Caucasian Scabious
Late summer flowers 2-3" (2.5-7.5cm) across. Cultivars in white, blues and lavenders. Gray-green foliage. Grows 18-30" (45-75cm).

S. columbaria cultivars (ko-lum-BAH-ri-a)
Compact plants grow 12-18" (30-45cm), need no staking. Abundant flowers open in spring, continue into fall. Useful for edging, in beds, borders, containers.
   'Butterfly Blue' (2000 Perennial Plant of the Year): Lacy blue flowers.
   'Pink Mist' (PP 8957): soft pink, fully double blossoms.

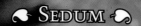

SEDUM (SEE-dum) ☀ ⋀⋀ 🌲 🦋
Stonecrop, Orpine

Easy succulents with fleshy leaves and clusters of blossoms that attract butterflies. Prefer fertile, well-drained soil though tolerant of infertile conditions. Many also tolerate drought and heat. Fine for rock garden and edging; use larger species and hybrids in borders.

Zones: 3-9, heat 8-3
Spacing: 18-24" (45-60cm)
Propagation: seed, division, cuttings (stem or leaf)

S. 'Matrona'
Hybrid with waxy, pink-edged gray-green leaves. Big clusters of soft pink flowers open in late summer. Grows 10-16" (25-40cm).

S. 'Vera Jameson'
Hybrid sedum with waxy, bluish to mahogany-red foliage and 4" (10cm) clusters of dusky pink. Grows 10-12" (25-30cm).

S. acre (AH-kree)
Golden-carpet, Goldmoss Stonecrop
Spreads vigorously with trailing stems. Mounds 2-3" (5-8cm) high. Useful filler between stepping or paving stones. Tiny pale green scale-like leaves cover stems. Spring flowers golden yellow. Naturalized.

S. album (AL-bum)
Wormgrass, White Stonecrop
Creeping spreader mounds 3-8" (8-20cm). Early summer white flowers in flat-topped clusters (panicles).

S. kamtschaticum (kamt-SHAT-i-kum)
Kamschatca Sedum/Stonecrop, Orange Stonecrop
Spreading, unbranched pale green stems bear 1½" (4cm) darker leaves that turn bronze in fall. Mounds 4-9" (10-23cm). Useful in dry walls. Summer flowers yellow to orange, in sparse flat clusters.
- subsp. *ellacombianum* (e-la-kom-bee-AH-num): scalloped leaf margins and bright yellow or lemon-yellow flowers on 4-6" (10-15cm) mounds.
- subsp. *middendorffianum* (mid-en-dorf-ee-AH-num): dark green, needle-like leaves and bright yellow flowers on 4-6" (10-15cm) mounds.

S. oreganum (o-ree-GAH-num)
Oregon Stonecrop
Clump-forming succulent with red-tinted foliage that turns completely red in hot climate. Height to 6" (15cm). Late spring yellow flowers fade to pale pink. Naturalized.

S. sieboldii (see-BOHL-dee-y)
October Daphne, October Plant
Spreading plant mounds 6-9" (15-23cm). Rounded 1" (2.5cm) leaves in groups of three on trailing stems. Late summer pink flowers. Early frost may prevent flowering. Good at front of borders.

S. spectabile (spek-TAH-bi-lee)
Showy Stonecrop, Showy Sedum
Clusters of showy red or pink flowers top attractive gray-green foliage in late summer. Grows 18-24" (45-60cm). Tolerates partial shade; grows in dry soil. Useful sedum for borders, edging.
- **'Autumn Joy':** grows to 24" (60cm) with densely clustered pink to rusty-red flowers; tolerates moist soils.
- **'Brilliant':** raspberry-red flowers on 18" (45cm) plants.

S. spurium (SPEW-ri-um)
Two-row Stonecrop
Vigorous spreader forms dense mats mounding 2-6" (5-15cm). Trailing reddish stems root readily, develop new ascending stem clusters. Grows in dry soil. Red-edged younger foliage turns deeper red in fall. White to rose summer flower clusters rise 4" (10cm) or more over leafy clumps. Good sedum for borders, edging; excellent groundcover.
- **'Bronze Carpet':** bronze foliage; to 4" (10cm) high; pink flowers.
- **'Dragon's Blood':** purplish foliage; plant grows 3-4" (8-10cm) high; flowers dark red.
- **'Fulda Glow':** Improved form of 'Dragon's Blood'.
- **'Red Carpet':** brilliant red foliage mounds 3-4" (8-10cm) high; red flowers.

Sedum acre

Sedum 'Matrona'

Sedum 'Vera Jameson'

Sedum album

Sedum kamtschaticum

Sedum kamtschaticum subsp.
ellacombianum

Sedum sieboldii

Sedum spectabile 'Autumn Joy'

Sedum spectabile 'Brilliant'

Sedum spurium 'Dragon's Blood'

SEMPERVIVUM (sem-per-VEE-vum)
Houseleek, Live-forever, Hen-and-chickens ☼ ⋙ ♠
Easy, adaptable stoloniferous succulents with symmetrical leafy rosettes and loose spikes of white, green, yellow, rosy, or purple summer blossom. Best in well-drained sandy or gritty soil. Useful in containers, rock or wall gardens, on stony banks, as groundcover. Rosettes die after flowering but are replaced by offsets. Many species and cultivars have green, red-marked, or entirely red foliage.
Zones: 3-8, heat 8-1
Spacing: 8-10" (20-25cm)
Propagation: division, seed

S. arachnoideum (a-rak-NOI-dee-um)
Spiderweb, Cobweb Houseleek
Dense webbing of gray threads over pale green leafy rosettes.

SIDALCEA (si-DAL-see-a) ☼ ✄
S. malviflora (mal-vi-FLOH-ra)
Checker-mallow, Prairie Mallow
Summer-flowering perennial with hollyhock-like blossom. Height ranges from 24" (60cm) to 5' (1.5m). Grows best in well-drained soil. Useful in borders, natural plantings. Foliage lobed, divided. White, rose, or pink flowers on branching spikes. Named garden varieties developed from native species. Naturalized.
Zones: 5-9, heat 8-2
Spacing: 24-30" (60-75cm)
Propagation: seed (species), division (hybrids, cultivars)

Sempervivum arachnoideum

Sempervivum

Sidalcea

Solidago hybrids (so-li-DAH-goh)

Goldenrod

Vigorous summer to fall-flowering perennials for informal borders and natural plantings. Cultivar heights 1-5' (0.3-1.5m); taller plants may need support. Good in moist, well-drained soil. Clusters of blossom in shades of yellow. Species readily self-seeding, may become invasive. Tolerates dry soil. Naturalized.

   'Golden Fleece': heart-shaped leaves, semi-evergreen; height to 18" (45cm). Listed as *S. sphacelata* cultivar.

Zones: 2-8, heat 9-6
Spacing: 18-24" (45-60cm)
Propagation: seed, division

XSolidaster (so-li-DAS-ter)

X*S. luteus* (LOO-tee-us)
[X*S. hybridus* (HYB-ri-dus)]
Hybrid Goldenrod
Intergeneric hybrid of Solidago and Aster produces clustered small yellow daisies from midsummer. Height 18-36" (30-90cm). Best in well-drained soil. Good in borders, natural plantings.
Zones: 2-8, heat 9-5
Spacing: 18-24" (45-60cm)
Propagation: division

Solidago

X*Solidaster luteus*

STACHYS (STAK-is)

Betony, Hedge Nettle, Woundwort
S. byzantina (bi-zan-TEE-na)
[*S. lanata* (la-NAH-ta)]
Woolly Betony, Lamb's-ears
Velvety spreading foliage forms mat 12-15" (30-38cm) high. Best in moist yet well-drained soil. Good edging, rock garden, groundcover plant. Big, white-woolly leaves resemble lamb's ears. Spikes of pink to purple flowers in spring. Tolerates shade in dry soil.
Zones: 4-8, heat 9-1
Spacing: 12-18" (30-45cm)
Propagation: seed, division

STOKESIA (STOHK-si-a, STOH-kee-si-a)

S. laevis (LEE-vis)
Stokes' Aster
Easily grown border plant provides year-round dark green foliage and 1-4" (2.5-10cm) blooms in summer. Height 12-24" (30-60cm). Best in sandy, well-drained soil. Plant in groups for best display. Flowers blue to purple, with named cultivars in white and shades of blue. Naturalized.
   'Blue Danube': deep blue.
   'Klaus Jelitto': pale blue.
   'Silver Moon': white.
Zones: 5-9, heat 8-4
Spacing: 12-15" (30-38cm)
Propagation: seed, division in spring

Stachys byzantina

Symphytum caucasicum

Stokesia laevis   *S. laevis* 'Silver Moon'

Tanacetum vulgare

Tanacetum coccineum

Tanacetum parthenium

SYMPHYTUM (SIM-fi-tum)

Comfrey

Vigorous clump-forming perennials suitable for natural planting or informal borders. Best in moist soils. Large basal leaves, smaller upper ones. Flowers borne in loose branching clusters.

Zones: 3-8, heat 9-4
Spacing: 12-24" (30-60cm)
Propagation: division, seed

S. caucasicum (kaw-KAS-i-kum)

Blue Comfrey

Upright plants with soft hairy foliage and spring flowers opening pink, then turning blue. Remove spent blooms to extend flowering. Grows 18-24" (45-60cm).

S. grandiflorum (gran-di-FLOH-rum) ᰧ

Large-flowered Comfrey, Groundcover Comfrey

Rapidly spreading rhizomatous plant with shiny leaves and stems that rise 10-15" (25-38cm). Spring flowers creamy-yellow. Tolerates dry conditions.

TANACETUM (ta-na-SEE-tum) ☼ ☁

Tansy

Easy-to-grow, hardy perennials for borders and massed plantings. Best in fertile well-drained soil. Leaves often aromatic. Flowers from daisy to button. Long-lasting when cut. Cut tops to the ground after killing frost in fall, and apply winter mulch in cold areas. When spring shoots are 6-8" (15-20cm) long, pinch tips to encourage bushiness. Divide in spring every 2-3 years.

Zones: see individual species for hardiness; heat 9-1
Spacing: 18-30" (45-75cm)
Propagation: division, seed

T. coccineum (kok-SIN-ee-um)

[Chrysanthemum coccineum]

Pyrethrum, Painted Daisy

Reliable early summer daisy blossoms. Flower petals of white, red or pink shades with yellow centers. Height 12-24" (30-60cm); taller plants may need support. Flowers single or double, 3" (8cm) across, on wiry stems above vivid green fern-like foliage. Cut back after flowering to encourage new growth and fall flowers. Best in cooler climates; protect from afternoon sun in southern zones. Zones 3-7.

T. parthenium (par-THEE-ni-um)

[Chrysanthemum parthenium]

Feverfew, Matricaria

Bushy plant for summer blossom, 12-36" (30-90cm) tall. Foliage is strongly aromatic. Button-like flowers, 3/4" (2cm) across, cover plants in mid to late summer. Zones 5-8.
  '**Golden Ball**': yellow flowers; height to 18" (45cm).
  '**Snowball**': white flowers; grows 24-36" (60-90cm) tall.

T. vulgare (vul-GAH-ree)

Common Tansy, Golden-buttons

Naturalized herb grown for its yellow button flowers and deeply cut, ferny, aromatic foliage. Height to 36" (90cm). Grows in any well-drained soil. Useful as border filler, in herb garden, natural planting. Flowers in summer. Zones 3-9.

Note: leaves and stems are poisonous.

t

TEUCRIUM (TEW-kri-um) ☼ ⋙ 🌲

Germander

T. chamaedrys (ka-MEE-dris)
Wall Germander

Compact, shrubby, aromatic evergreen with shiny oval leaves. Height 10-15" (25-38cm). Best in moist yet well-drained soil. Useful as low hedge, at front of border, for edging. Shear or trim for formal shape. Late summer flowers rose-purple. Tolerates some shade.

  'Prostratum' (pros-TRAH-tum): good groundcover plant, growing 6-10" (15-25cm) high. Rose-pink flowers.

Zones: 4-9, heat 12-4
Spacing: 6-18" (15-45cm)
Propagation: seed, division

For added weed control under mulch, first spread two or three sheets of newspaper (not color or glossy sections) over the soil surface. Then apply the mulch.

Teucrium chamaedrys

Teucrium chamaedrys 'Prostratum'

THALICTRUM (tha-LIK-trum) ☼ ☁ ✂

Meadow Rue

Elegant plants with airy divided foliage and fluffy blossoms in late spring and summer. Best in moist, rich soil. Useful light contrast in borders, for edge of woodland, close to water.

Zones: 5-8, heat 9-1
Spacing: 24-30" (60-75cm)
Propagation: seed, division

T. aquilegifolium (ak-wi-lee-ji-FOH-li-um)
Columbine Meadow Rue

Clump-forming with masses of blue-green leaves. Height 24-36" (60-90cm). Late spring lilac-blue flowers in 6-8" (15-20cm) clusters. Cultivars have white, orange-tinged, or blue-purple blossoms. Male and female flowers on separate plants. Tolerates heat.

T. delavayi (de-la-VAY-y)
and **T. dipterocarpum** (dip-te-roh-KAR-pum)
Yunnan Meadow Rue

Graceful, slender stems rise 2-4' (0.6-1.2m). Fern-like foliage. Airy, lilac-and-cream to mauve flower clusters in summer. Provide support for flowering stems.

T. dioicum (dy-OH-i-kum)
Early Meadow Rue

Dainty native for natural plantings in moist locations. Height 12-24" (30-60cm). Early summer blossoms creamy-white, in 12" (30cm) fluffy clusters. Male and female flowers on separate plants.

T. rochebrunianum (roh-sheh-brew-nee-AH-num)
Lavender Mist Meadow Rue

Hardy, vigorous plants grow 4-5' (1.2-1.5m) tall. Airy, lavender pink summer blossoms have golden yellow stamens, contrast well with blue-green foliage. Performs best in partial shade. Hardy to zone 3.

Thalictrum dipterocarpum

Thermopsis caroliniana

Thymus X*citriodorus*

Thymus serpyllum

THERMOPSIS (ther-MOP-sis) ☼ ✂

False Lupine

T. caroliniana (ka-ro-li-nee-AH-na)
[*T. villosa* (vil-LOH-sa)]
Carolina Lupine
Long-lived, sprawling perennial has yellow spring flow-
ers on compact, upright spikes resembling lupines.
Height $2^1/_2$-4' (0.75-1.2m). Good in border, natural plant-
ing. Leaves blue-green, divided. Tolerates some shade.
Resists drought. Naturalized.
Zones: 3-9, heat 8-1
Spacing: 24-36" (60-90cm)
Propagation: division in spring, seed, sown as soon as
                 ripe in late summer

THYMUS (TY-mus) ☼ ⛅ ⌇ 🌲

Thyme
Low-growing aromatic herbs with shrubby, sprawling
and upright stems. Best in light, well-drained, acid soil.
Useful in rock garden, herb garden, as edging, and as
groundcover for banks and no-traffic areas. Small, shiny
oval leaves. Rose or lilac flowers in early summer.
Zones: 4-8, heat 9-1
Spacing: 10-12" (25-30cm)
Propagation: seed, division

T. Xcitriodorus (sit-ree-o-DOH-rus)
Lemon Thyme
Many-branched, semi-trailing plant grows 6-12"
(15-30cm) high. Lemon scented. Tiny leaves, pale purple
flowers. Cut back in spring to encourage fresh compact
growth. Zones 5-8.

T. pseudolanuginosus (soo-doh-la-new-gi-NOH-sus)
Woolly Thyme
Sprawling shrubby evergreen forms undulating mat 2-4"
(5-10cm) high. Gray woolly foliage covers stems. Pinkish flowers rare.

T. serpyllum (ser-PIL-lum)
Mother-of-thyme, Wild Thyme
Rooting, spreading stems with small upright branches
form mat 2-6" (5-15cm) high. Roundish, dark green
leaves, used for seasoning and in pot-pourri. Small pur-
plish-white flower clusters in summer.

Thymus pseudolanuginosus

TIARELLA (tee-a-REL-a)
False Miterwort
T. cordifolia (kor-di-FOH-li-a)
Foamflower, Allegheny Foamflower
Low maintenance groundcover for shade and rich, moist soils. Foliage provides foil for profuse clusters of spring or summer flowers. Lobed, heart-shaped leaves have burgundy coloring along veins in spring and fall, may turn entirely bronze in winter. Rapidly spreading stoloniferous plants mound 6-12" (15-30cm) high. Delicate pink flower buds open to long-lasting creamy-white spring flowers. Naturalized.
> **T. cordifolia var. collina** (ko-LEE-na) [*T. wherryi* (WE-ree-y)], Wherry's Foamflower: foliage turns reddish in winter. Slower to spread than species, clump-forming, mounds 4-10" (10-25cm). White, airy flowers in summer.

Zones: 3-8, heat 8-4
Spacing: 12-30" (30-75cm)
Propagation: division, seed

TRADESCANTIA (tra-des-KAN-shi-a)
T. virginiana (vir-ji-nee-AH-na)
Spiderwort, Widow's-tears
Reliable, grass-like perennial for borders, natural plantings, partly shaded woodland locations. Stems sprawl and rise to 12-24" (30-60cm). Prefers fertile, well-drained soil. Tolerates dry conditions. Short-lived flowers in white and shades of blue to purple open from late spring to midsummer. Naturalized.
Zones: 3-9, heat 12-1
Spacing: 24-30" (60-75cm)
Propagation: division in spring, seed

TRICYRTIS (try-KUR-tis)
Toad Lily
T. hirta (HIR-ta)
Toad Lily, Hairy Toad Lily, Japanese Toad Lily
Late summer or fall flowering rhizomatous lily, 24-36" (60-90cm) high. Best in rich, moist yet well-drained soil. Good in border, rock garden, container. Arching stems clothed with soft-hairy foliage. Flowers white to lilac with darker spots and blotches.
Zones: 4-8, heat 9-6
Spacing: 18-24" (45-60cm)
Propagation: division in spring, seed

Tiarella cordifolia var. *collina*

Tradescantia virginiana

Tricyrtis hirta

Trillium grandiflorum

Trollius chinensis

Verbena canadensis

TRILLIUM (TRIL-i-um)

T. grandiflorum (gran-di-FLOH-rum)
Snow Trillium, Wake-robin, Great White Trillium
Showy three-petaled spring flowers top leafy 9-18" (23-45cm) stems. Must have rich, moist soil and at least partial shade. Plant in woodland, shaded border, or natural area. Flower opens white, fades to pink and rose. Clump-forming. Plant rhizomes about 4" (10cm) deep. Naturalized.
Zones: 4-9, heat 8-1
Spacing: 16-20" (40-50cm)
Propagation: division, seed (slow to germinate)

TROLLIUS (TROL-i-us)

Globeflower
T. chinensis (chi-NEN-sis)
[*T. ledebourii* (le-de-BOOR-ee-y)]
Ledebour Globeflower
Large orange buttercup flowers in spring on 24-36" (60-90cm) stems. Best in moist, heavy soil and cool climate. Useful in boggy meadow, natural planting, shaded border, at edge of pond or stream. Deep-cut leaves mound under flowering stems. Vigorous.
Zones: 3-7, heat 8-3
Spacing: 20-30" (50-75cm)
Propagation: seed, division

VERBENA (ver-BEE-na)

V. canadensis hybrids (ka-na-DEN-sis)
Vervain
Free-flowering, tender perennials with showy flowers, developed from native species. Tolerate heat and drought. Mounds rise 6-12" (15-30cm). Clusters of flowers open from summer to fall; colors range from blue-purples to lavenders, reds and pinks, to white and multi-toned. Best growth in well-drained soils. Useful as edging, in rock garden, containers. Spreads by creeping, rooting stems. Naturalized.
Zones: 8-11, heat 12-1
Spacing: 24-30" (45-60cm)
Propagation: cuttings, seed

Veronica spicata

VERONICA (ve-RON-i-ka)

Speedwell, Brooklime

Clump-forming or spreading perennials with blue, white, or rose flowers in clusters or spikes. Best in well-drained soil. Useful plants for border, edging, rock garden, groundcover, or for cutting. Remove faded blossoms to encourage more flower development.

Zones: see individual species for hardiness; heat 8-2
Spacing: 12-18" (30-45cm)
Propagation: division, cuttings, seed (species)

V. 'Goodness Grows': violet blue flowers open from April to frost. Compact plant grows 10-12" (25-30cm). Zones 3-8.

V. 'Sunny Border Blue' (1993 Perennial Plant of the Year): violet blue flower spikes rise 18-20" (45-50cm), summer to early fall. Rounded, dark green leaves. Zones 3-8.

V. austriaca (aws-tri-AH-ka)
[*V. latifolia* (la-ti-FOH-li-a), *V. spicata* (spee-KAH-ta), *V. teucrium* (TEW-kri-um)]
Hungarian Speedwell
Spreading groundcover grows 6-20" (15-50cm) high. Zones 3-8.
  'Crater Lake Blue': compact form with bright blue flowers; height 12-15" (30-38cm).

V. incana (in-KAH-na)
Woolly Speedwell
Silvery-gray woolly foliage and stems, blue summer flowers. Height 12-18" (30-45cm). Intolerant of extreme heat or humidity. Zones 3-7.

V. longifolia (lon-ji-FOH-li-a)
[*V. maritima* (ma-RIT-i-ma)]
Long-leaf Veronica
Clump-forming, naturalized species has smooth stems, grows to 2-4' (0.6-1.2m). Useful in border and for cutting. Lilac flowers on 12" (30cm) spikes in summer. Zones 4-8.

V. prostrata (pros-TRAH-ta)
[*V. rupestris* (roo-PES-tris)]
Harebell Speedwell
Dense, mat-forming plant with flowering stems rising to 8" (20cm) over gray-green foliage. Blue spring flower clusters. Zones 5-8.

V. repens (REE-penz)
Creeping Speedwell
Prostrate stems form mound 4" (10cm) high. Moss-like, lustrous foliage. White, rose or bluish spring flowers in small groups. Zones 5-8.

V. spicata (spee-KAH-ta)
Spike Speedwell
Clump-forming, grows to 10-36" (25-90cm). Glossy foliage. Blue flowers in dense 12-36" (30-90cm) spikes. Varieties flower in white, shades of blue, and pink. Zones 3-8.
  'Blue Charm': uniform plants 18-30" (45-75cm) tall, 15-30" (38-75cm) across. Abundant lavender blue flowers all summer.

Veronica 'Goodness Grows'

Veronica 'Sunny Border Blue'

Veronica austriaca 'Crater Lake Blue'

Veronica prostrata

Veronica repens 'Alba'

Veronica spicata

VINCA (VIN-ka)
Periwinkle
Spreading, trailing woody vines bear glossy dark green leaves. Grows in any well-drained soil, dies back in drought. Useful container plant, groundcover for shaded areas such as banks, edging. Shearing encourages dense growth. Flowers freely in sun, from early spring.
Zones: see individual species
Spacing: 12-24" (30-60cm)
Propagation: division, layers, cuttings, seed

V. major (MAY-jor)
Greater Periwinkle, Blue-buttons, Band Plant
Tender creeper for warm climate groundcover, does well in protected locations and seasonal containers in the north. Mounds 12-18" (30-45cm). Large 2-3" (5-8cm) leaves. Bright blue to purple flowers. Hardiness zones 7-11, heat 12-7.
    'Variegata': foliage variegated green and yellow.

V. minor (MY-nor)
Common Periwinkle, Myrtle
Prostrate stems root as they spread. Plants cover area with mass of elliptical, 1$^{1}/_{2}$" (4cm), shiny green leaves. Vigorous and tolerant naturalized perennial has cultivars with white, blue, or purple flowers, some with variegated foliage. Hardiness zones 4-10, heat 9-1. Naturalized.

Vinca minor

Vinca minor

Viola cornuta

Viola obliqua

Viola odorata

VIOLA (VY-oh-la) ☼ ⛅ ✂
Violet

Low-growing, tufted or clump-forming perennials with distinctive fragrant flowers in spring. Prefer moist, well-drained soil. Useful as edging, on banks, in rock garden, natural planting, moist woodland sites.
Zones: hardiness 4-9, may vary by species; heat 12-1
Spacing: 6-12" (15-30cm)
Propagation: division, seed

V. canadensis (ka-na-DEN-sis)
Canada Violet
Fragrant purple-tinged white flowers with yellow eye. Height to 12" (30cm). Best in shaded location. Hardy to zone 3. Naturalized.

V. cornuta (kor-NEW-ta) 🌲
Horned Violet, Viola, Tufted Pansy
Spring flowers violet-blue; cultivars have larger flowers in white, yellow, apricot, red, and purple shades. Main stems tend to sprawl and mound to 4-12" (10-30cm). Cut back after flowering to encourage second bloom in fall-winter. Vigorous tender perennial grown as annual bedding plant in all zones. Perennial and evergreen in zones 6-9.

V. obliqua (oh-BLEE-ka)
[*V. cucullata* (koo-kew-LAH-ta)]
Marsh Blue Violet
Violet flowers rise 3-6" (8-15cm). Pale, undulating leaves are 3-4" (8-10cm) wide. Tufted growth from scaly rhizomes. Several cultivars. Naturalized.

V. odorata (oh-do-RAH-ta) 〰
Sweet Violet, Garden Violet, English Violet
Fragrant spring flowers are violet, rose, or white. Height 2-8" (5-20cm). Broad oval or kidney-shaped leaves. Spreads rapidly with long runners. Self-seeding; semi-evergreen. Zones 6-8.

V. pedata (pe-DAH-ta)
Bird-foot Violet, Pansy Violet, Crowfoot Violet
Clump-forming, mounds 2-6" (5-15cm) high. Needs well-drained, sandy soil and shade. Leaves palmately divided, like birds' feet. Two upper petals are dark purple, lower three are pale lilac. Varieties have white or violet blossoms. Naturalized.

V. pubescens (pew-BES-enz)
Downy Yellow Violet
Softly hairy stems and foliage, with most leaves near stem tips. Height 8-12" (20-30cm). Bright yellow flowers in spring. Best in rich dry soil, shade, and cooler climates of zones 3-7. Naturalized.

☼ = Full Sun   ✂ = Cut Flowers
⛅ = Partial Sun/Shade   🌲 = Evergreen
☁ = Shade   🦋 = attracts Butterflies
〰 = Groundcover   ✦ = attracts Hummingbirds

WALDSTEINIA (vald-STY-ni-a) ☼ ⛅ ☁ 〰

Easy-to-grow, spreading strawberry-like groundcovers with dry, inedible fruits. Yellow flowers in late spring, early summer. Best in well-drained soil. Useful in rock gardens, as groundcover. Creeping rhizomes, semi-evergreen foliage.

Zones: 4-7
Spacing: 12-20" (30-50cm)
Propagation: division

W. fragarioides (fra-gah-ree-OI-deez)
Barren Strawberry
Forms spreading mat 4-6" (10-15cm) high. Naturalized.

W. ternata (ter-NAH-ta)
[*W. trifolia* (try-FOH-li-a)]
Siberian Barren Strawberry
Compact and spreading. Neat leafy rosettes rise to 4" (10cm). Useful for groundcover on banks.

YUCCA (YOO-ka) ☼ ⬆

Stemless or short-stemmed shrubs provide year-round value as accent in dry border or as single or grouped specimens. Best in well-drained sandy loam. Dramatic, sword-like succulent leaves in basal rosette from which rise showy clusters of fragrant white or creamy blossoms in summer. Naturalized.

Zones: 4-10, heat 9-1
Spacing: 3-5' (0.9-1.5m)
Propagation: seed, offsets

Y. filamentosa (fi-la-men-TOH-sa)
Adam's-needle, Spoonleaf Yucca
Leafy rosette grows to 36" (90cm). Arching flower stems usually rise 4-5' (1.2-1.5m), sometimes as high as 15' (4.5m). Creamy-white, pendulous blossoms.

Y. glauca (GLAW-ka)
Soapweed
Short, prostrate stems give rise to clumps of pale green foliage rising to 36" (90cm). Leaves have white or brown margins. Greenish-white flowers in 30" (75cm) clusters.

Waldsteinia ternata

Yucca filamentosa